PROTECTING ASSETS WITH ESTATE PLANNING

WILLS, TRUSTS,

AND OTHER

LEGAL OPTIONS

DONALD J. BURRIS, ESQ.

Makai Publishing Group
Scottsdale, Arizona

Library of Congress Catalog Card Number: 93-77885
ISBN 0-9630356-5-7
Author, Donald J. Burris
Printed in the United States of America

Cover design by Cindy Mackey, CM Design Groupe, Phoenix

Layman's LawGuides is a division of
Makai Publishing Group
P.O. Box 14213
Scottsdale, AZ 85267-4213

Produced by Ronald Adamson, Sacramento

———————————————

Instead of writing combinations of the pronouns "he" and "she" as he or she, he/she, s/he, we have elected to use the word "he" uniformly throughout this book when identifying a person. The use of "he" is not meant to be offensive, but is written for the sake of convenience and consistency.

ACKNOWLEGEMENTS

I wish to acknowledge the hard work, fine effort and excellent writing ability of my daughter Angela L. Vehorn. Without her efforts, this book would not have been made.

Donald J. Burris

TABLE OF CONTENTS

CHAPTER SIX:
IS IT TRUST-WORTHY?

CHAPTER SEVEN:
WHAT YOU NEED TO KNOW ABOUT ESTATE TAXES

CHAPTER EIGHT:
UNDERSTANDING THE LIVING TRUST

INTRODUCTION:
WHICH ESTATE PLAN IS BEST FOR ME?

Patrick Fullerman, a successful business-man and father of four, marched into the office of Brown and Brown, financial advisors, one Thursday afternoon. Patrick had seen an advertisement for the firm on a billboard while driving down the freeway. "Keep your money in your family," it had said. "Call Brown and Brown, estate planning specialists." The ad caught Patrick's eye because he did not want his estate to end up like his father's, with almost half the assets going to the IRS. Patrick wondered if there was a way to make sure his assets will go to whom he desires, when he desires, with minimal taxation, when he dies. He had heard so many differing viewpoints. Would a simple will suffice? Does he need a trust, and, if so, what kind? Which tax-saving methods are best for his circumstances? Furthermore, how does he know if Brown and Brown has the right answers?

> *Your estate plan determines how much of the assets of your estate will go to taxes and attorneys.*

Most likely you, like Patrick Fullerman, care deeply about your family and want to make sure the assets you have worked so hard for will go to them when you die. Since your estate plan determines how much of the assets of your estate will go to taxes and attorneys rather than to your family and the friends and institutions of your choice, it is imperative that you take the time to consider which estate plan is best for you. It is also vital that you choose an experienced estate planning attorney. An experienced attorney can create an estate plan that suits your needs. Non specialists, attorneys or otherwise, may be unfamiliar with the law, using forms that are not specifically tailored to your needs.

To help you to make an informed decision, this book is designed to help you accomplish the following ten goals:

- Maximize control of your estate
- Maximize access to your estate
- Maximize preservation of your estate
- Maximize proper management of your estate
- Maximize privacy of your estate
- Minimize time of estate settlement
- Minimize complexity of estate settlement
- Minimize costs
- Minimize taxes
- Minimize time of distribution

If these ten goals are met successfully, you will be able to minimize the negative consequences and maximize efficiency and effectiveness. In order to do this, you must first be aware of the available alternatives for estate planning. Basically, there are four ways for property to pass to recipients:

1. Intestate succession
2. Joint tenancy and tenancy by the entirety
3. Wills
4. Trusts

CHAPTER ONE: INTESTATE SUCCESSION— THE UNPLANNED RESULT

Jeremy Newton was a successful contractor with a loving wife and three children. At thirty-five, he figured, "I'm a young, healthy guy, so I'll wait till later to create an estate plan. Besides, when I die, it's simple: my assets will go to my wife and kids, right?" Wrong! As his family was about to discover, the law is not that simple. When Jeremy tragically was killed in a work-related accident, his affairs were far from being in order. After enduring a lengthy (not to mention costly) probate process, Jeremy's assets were not distributed in the way he intended. Because he did not leave a written account of his wishes, the court was free to determine who would receive what and when.

> *If you do not leave a written account of your wishes, the court is free to determine who receives what and when.*

Consequences of an Intestate Estate

Unfortunately, such situations are not uncommon. The most common method of estate planning today is to do nothing, which results in an intestate estate. This means your estate will pass to your heirs under the intestate succession laws of your state. Your estate may be required to go through probate, an expensive, time-consuming process, both upon your death and the death of your spouse. The laws of the state determine to whom your estate will be transferred. The court picks the person who will administer the probate of your estate. This means that neither you, nor your family, will choose who will be in control of your affairs. The state may appoint a total stranger to administer your probate estate! In most states, the probate codes direct that the entire estate will pass to the spouse and children, with varying proportions to each.

With this plan (or lack of planning), the laws of the state of your residence will normally dictate who is to receive your property. Many times the heirs to whom you would have left the property are not the same as those determined by the state. In some states, half of your assets may go to your children, rather than your surviving spouse. Minor children may have to have a conservator or guardian appointed for them through the probate court. In such a case, the conservator would have to account to a court on a periodic basis for money spent on the children's behalf. An attorney may have to be involved throughout the existence of the conservatorship or guardianship.

Many times the heirs to whom you would have left the property are not the some as those determined by the state.

If your surviving spouse remarries, the new husband or wife may be entitled to your spouse's inheritance, with no obligation to use anything on behalf of your children. Because your family members are not receiving the funds to which they feel they are entitled, intestate succession could result in a contest or dispute between them.

Intestate succession is the easiest plan for you, because it means you, while you are alive, do nothing. And you don't spend anything! But it may be costly to your heirs, both in terms of expense and distribution to the wrong people.

SUMMARY

With intestate succession, the laws of the state

determine to whom your estate will be transferred, with no guarantee that the property will be distributed to the desired heirs. Possible result: A contest or dispute between heirs.

CHAPTER TWO:
JOINT TENANCY AND TENANCY BY THE ENTIRETY

• •

How Do They Compare?

Joint tenancy and tenancy by the entirety are both merely methods of holding title to assets. Joint tenancy can be held by two or more individuals regardless of marital status and tenancy by the entirety is limited to married couples. Joint tenancy may be terminated by any joint tenant. Tenancy by the entirety, on the other hand, may be terminated only by the joint action of both owners during their lifetimes. Most states have repealed tenancy by the entirety.

The Consequences of Joint Tenancy

Joint tenancy is the most common method of holding title to assets, particularly family residences. It is often used to avoid the probate process upon the death of the first tenant. However, property held in joint tenancy in most instances will have to go through probate upon the death of the joint tenant last to die. To designate joint tenancy, the words "joint tenancy with right of survivorship" should appear on the title document of the asset. Generally speaking, joint tenancy may be an appropriate planning device for a married couple. With few exceptions, however, joint tenancy is inadvisable with anyone else.

> *Joint tenancy is the most common method of holding title to assets, particularly family residences.*

Disadvantages of Joint Tenancy

Holding assets in joint tenancy with anyone can have several disadvantages. Suppose you decide to hold your home and bank account in joint tenancy with your son, Johnny. After obtaining his driver's license, Johnny goes out with some buddies on a snowy Friday night, hits a patch of ice, and ends up plowing through somebody's living room. The owners of the newly air conditioned home take Johnny to court, resulting in a sizable judgment against him. Since Johnny is a joint tenant to your home and bank account, each could be considered part of his estate. His share could be lost as the result of such judgment.

Other problems may result. Under current law, you can gift up to $10,000 per person, per calendar year, tax free. However, you must file a gift tax return if you gift in excess of that amount to any individual. So if you own a home worth $100,000 and you place it in joint tenancy with your son, Johnny, you effectively have gifted him $50,000. Although $10,000 is exempted from gift taxes, the remaining $40,000 may be subject to a gift tax. Although there may not be any gift tax, filing a gift tax return is then required, and significant penalties may result if this is not done. Remember, under current law, you may gift any amount to your spouse without any gift taxes and without the need to file a gift tax return.

You can gift up to $10,000 per person, per calendar year, tax free.

Suppose at a later date Johnny is forced to file bankruptcy. Then the trustee for the bankruptcy can sell Johnny's interest in the home. Or, if he goes through a divorce, his wife may be entitled to part of his joint tenancy share.

In other words, by placing Johnny's name on the home as a joint tenant, you have made yourself vulnerable for his financial difficulties.

You may have control problems, too, by placing property in joint tenancy with anyone. If your name alone is on the title, in most cases it will take just your signature to sell or transfer the asset. But if you have the name of another on the title in joint tenancy, that person's signature will probably be required as well. If you put Johnny's name as joint tenant on the title to your home, he has to sign the deed if you want to sell it, or the mortgage if you want to take out a loan against it. And if he doesn't want to, you can't do it! The same may apply for securities and other property.

By placing someone's name on the home as a joint tenant, you have made yourself vulnerable to their financial difficulties.

The Benefits of Stepped-up Valuation

There is yet another reason not to enter into joint tenancy with just anyone. Remember, you effectively gift to the other joint tenant a share of the property placed in joint tenancy. As a gift, the value of the share is received at your cost basis, usually the purchase price when you bought it. This should not make any difference income tax-wise if you sell the property while you are alive. But if you die, and the fair market value of the property at the time of your death is substantially more, more income taxes may have to be paid when the property is sold later. You see, the value for income tax purposes "steps up" to the date of death value or "steps down" if the date of death value is less than your cost basis. If the property is owned in joint tenancy, only your share receives the stepped-up (or stepped-down) valuation as of the date of your death.

For example, imagine you purchased a home in 1975 for $80,000 (the cost basis). You put the home in joint tenancy with your spouse. By the time of your death in an auto accident in 1993, the property value had risen to $200,000. Your half of the home would receive the stepped-up valuation. Thus, the value of your half rises from $40,000 to $100,000. However, your spouse's half of the home does not receive stepped-up valuation. So that half remains valued at the cost basis of $40,000. Suppose your spouse were to decide to sell the home, which now has a cost basis of $140,000, for the market value of $200,000. He or she would realize a taxable gain of $60,000! This disadvantage would be eliminated if the $125,000 once-in-a-lifetime home capital gain exclusion is used by your spouse.

EXAMPLE	1975	1991
Market Value	$80,000	$200,000
Your Half	$40,000	$100,000
Spouse's Half	$40,000	$40,000
Cost Basis	$80,000	$140,000
Taxable Gain	$0	$60,000

JOINT TENANCY:

- May be appropriate between spouses

- Inappropriate between anyone else

"The Survivor Takes All"

The concept of "the survivor takes all" may not present a problem if the joint tenants are husband and wife. However, imagine the situation if you and your spouse and your best friends, a husband and wife, decide to purchase a vacation home in Montana together. You place the home in joint tenancy with your friends. If you and your spouse were to die, your friends would own the entire home, rather than your heirs. Even if you had stated in your will whom you desired your share of the home to go to, joint tenancy takes precedence over a will.

Transfer Costs

Although joint tenancy avoids probate upon the death of the first spouse, it does not avoid legal costs at that time. Fees to have the attorney transfer the assets into the name of the survivor, fees for contesting, determining death taxes, reregistering jointly owned property in the sole name of the survivor, recording fees, fees for establishing the rights to joint bank accounts, etc., all need to be paid. And, upon the death of the last surviving joint tenant, that asset held in joint tenancy will probably have to go through probate of that joint tenant's estate and go to his or her heirs.

Joint tenancy avoids probate upon the death of the first tenant.

SUMMARY

- Joint tenancy can exist with any two or more individuals but tenancy by the entirety can exist only between spouses.

- Joint tenancy avoids probate upon the death of the first tenant.

- Holding property in joint tenancy can result in loss of control.

- Since joint tenancy is considered gifting, gift taxes may result.

- Property held in joint tenancy probably will have to go through probate upon the death of the tenant last to die.

- The benefits of stepped-up valuation may be reduced when you hold an asset in joint tenancy.

- Joint tenancy takes precedence over a will.

CHAPTER THREE:
COMMUNITY PROPERTY
AND SEPARATE PROPERTY
••

What's the Difference?

If you are married, your assets are considered by law either to be community property or separate property. There are eight original community property states: Arizona, California, Idaho, Louisiana, Nevada, New Mexico, Texas, and Washington. Wisconsin has recently adopted the community property concept. Some state legislatures are considering declaring their states to be community property states due to some tax advantages.

Community Property States

In states that recognize community property, all property attained before marriage is separate property. Property that one spouse receives by gift or inheritance during the marriage is also separate property. The other spouse has no claim to such separate property. Any other property acquired during marriage is community property, one-half being owned by each spouse.

> *In states that recognize community property, all property attained before marriage is separate property.*

Separate Property States

What about states that do not recognize community property? These separate property states generally consider property acquired by a married couple to be owned the way it is titled. Since property typically is titled in the name of the husband, separate property states generally assume that the husband holds sole title to all property.

Tax Consequences: Community vs. Separate

One tax advantage for owning property in a community property state is the benefit of stepped-up valuation upon the death of a spouse. Suppose a husband and wife were to purchase a house in a community property state for a cost basis of $80,000, with a market value of $200,000 upon the first death. The entire cost basis receives stepped-up valuation to that $200,000. If the surviving spouse were to sell the home for $200,000, the taxable gain would be zero. That is quite a difference from the $60,000 taxable gain if the home were held in joint tenancy! Remember, joint tenancy takes precedence over a will. It likewise takes precedence over the principles governing community property for tax purposes. If an asset is owned in joint tenancy between spouses, the surviving spouse may have a community property share of that asset under state law. But under federal tax law, only one-half of that asset can receive the date of death valuation, unless the spouses agree in writing otherwise. The other half retains original cost basis.

One tax advantage for owning property in a community property state is the benefit of stepped-up valuation upon the death of a spouse.

Suppose an asset is held as separate property in the name of either the husband or the wife. Then very different tax consequences would occur. If the husband owns it and he is the first to die, the cost basis would be changed to the fair market value as of the date of his death. It would be "stepped-up" if the value has gone up. If the wife later sells the asset, her income tax basis is the fair market value as of the date of her husband's death.

However, if the wife dies first, the results are very different. The property is separate property held in her husband's name. So she legally does not own any of the property. The husband would retain the property with the original cost basis. He would then lose the benefit of any change in valuation. Depending upon how much the value of the property had increased, a sizable taxable gain would result if he were to sell the property.

SUMMARY

- In community property states, all property obtained prior to marriage and property that one spouse receives by gift or inheritance during marriage is separate property.

- Other property acquired during marriage is community property.

- In separate property states, all property acquired by a married couple is normally considered to be owned the way it is titled.

- Joint tenancy can take precedence over the principles governing community property.

CHAPTER FOUR:
CAN YOU RELATE TO PROBATE?
· ·

Probate, simply stated, is the administration of your estate by a court. Your "estate" includes any assets that are owned in such a way by you that they must be probated to pass to your heirs. This includes assets that are owned in your name alone or in tenancy in common with someone else. That is, your share as a "tenant in common" with the other named individual or individuals is the share that is subject to probate upon your death, as the share or shares of the other named tenants in common would be subject to probate when each of them dies. Assets held in joint tenancy are not subject to probate when there is a surviving joint tenant. Assets that have a named beneficiary, such as an insurance policy or a retirement account, avoid probate.

Do you want 10% to 70% of your estate siphoned by probate fees and taxes?

Do you want 10-70% of your estate siphoned by probate fees and taxes? Some estates involved in a recent study by the Estate Research Institute were chopped in half by such costs. A county bar association surveyed 23,000 attorneys regarding probate costs. They found that 8-10% of the gross estate goes to probate fees. The amount of time for the probate process to be completed can be anywhere from 1½-2 years or even 3 or 4 years!

PROBATE FEES (estimates)

GROSS ESTATE	ATTORNEY'S FEES
$100,000	$3,000
$200,000	$5,000
$300,000	$7,000
$500,000	$11,000
$1,000,000	$21,000

Do you want everyone to have access to a list of your family's holdings and debts? That may happen with the probate process. If you are leaving a family business to your heirs, probate may expose business records to competitors and creditors as well. If privacy is an important factor in your estate plan, avoiding probate is vital.

Probate Process

To help you understand why the probate process is so lengthy, consider what is involved: a) gathering material and filing a petition with the court; b) publishing notice to creditors; c) inventorying assets and obtaining appraisals; d) preparing the accounting of assets and expenditures and filing a petition for the distribution and accounting; and e) filing the closing petition. It may be necessary to have one or more hearings in court during this process. Normally, it is necessary to also prepare income tax returns for the last partial year of life, income tax returns for the probate estate, and it may be necessary to prepare an estate tax return. Typical amounts of time necessary to complete these steps is as follows:

Gathering material and filing
petition .... 4-8 weeks

Publishing notice to creditors .... 4-6 months

Gathering assets, preparing
inventory, obtaining appraisals 1week-1year

Preparing accounting for assets
and expenditures, filing petition
for distribution and accounting .... 2-6 months

Filing closing petition .... 1-3 months

The amount of time it takes to complete this process depends upon the amount of work required in gathering the assets, obtaining signatures, finding locations of beneficiaries, as well as other procedures. It is difficult to close the estate in less than one year, and three years is not unreasonable.

The following chart indicates California's probate fees, as set by law, which are about average among states. These fees include compensation to the attorney and to the personal representative (called the "executor" in some states). If the personal representative does not take any compensation because he or she is already a beneficiary, then these amounts would be reduced by one-half. These fees do not include special fees for the sale of assets, tax preparation and litigation.

It is difficult to close the estate in less than one year, and four years is not unreasonable.

ASSETS	MINIMUM FEES
$ 200,000	$ 10,300
300,000	14,300
400,000	18,300
500,000	22,300
750,000	32,300
1,000,000	42,300
2,000,000	62,300
3,000,000	82,300
5,000,000	122,300

Obviously, the probate system is rather complex. There have been attempts to simplify the system, such as the Uniform Probate Code. To date, about 12 states have adopted all or part of the Uniform Probate Code, which is a good faith effort by attorneys to simplify probate procedures. The reality, though, is that the cost, time and complexity have been little affected.

Ancillary Proceedings

Separate probate proceedings may be necessary to open in any state where real property is located.

Separate probate proceedings may be necessary to open in any state where real property is located, depending upon how it is owned. If you have a home in Arizona and own a summer home in northern Minnesota, also in your name alone, probate in both states will be necessary upon your death. This means your family will have to endure the time and cost of two probates.

Ways to Avoid Probate

There are three basic ways to avoid the probate process: 1) joint tenancy (discussed in Chapter 2), which does not avoid probate when all of the named joint tenants die; 2) small estates (in most states, less than $60,000 in personal property and no real estate); and 3) the living trust.

THREE EXCEPTIONS TO PROBATE:

- Joint Tenancy

- Small Estates

- Living Trust

SUMMARY

- Probate is the process of eliminating claimants of your estate and transferring title.

- If privacy is important to you, avoiding

probate is vital.

- Probate is a time-consuming, costly, complicated process.

- It may be necessary to open up probate proceedings in each state where real property is located.

CHAPTER FIVE:
WHERE THERE IS A WILL,
THERE IS A WAY

Simply defined, a will is a legally enforceable, written declaration of a person's intended distribution of property after death. A will is revocable (which means it can be terminated) during the creator's lifetime. It takes effect only upon death. Generally, state statutes control the right and power to execute a will. They also set the procedure that must be followed. Although these statutes are not uniform in all fifty states, they are basically similar. The four basic required elements for properly executing a will are discussed below.

1. *Capacity of the testate (creator of the will)*

Can anyone create a legally valid will? No. For one thing, all states require the testate to be of majority age, normally eighteen. So little Annie scribbling on a piece of paper whom she wants her dolls to go to when she dies doesn't count. Secondly, a person must be sane. This means he or she must possess the soundness of mind to have sufficient mental capacity to understand the extent of property owned, as well as the effect of a will in disposing of such property. A testate must be able to use these facts to make a rational judgment. Granted, we all have days we would not meet these requirements, but you get the idea.

> *A will is a legally enforceable, written declaration of a person's intended distribution of property after death.*

2. The form of the will

A will usually must be either written, printed or typed. A handwritten, or holographic, will is valid only if it meets all other formal requirements unless otherwise provided by statute. State statutes must be reviewed to determine such a will's validity.

Suppose Aunt Matilda, with no formal written will, bequeaths you all her property on her deathbed. A few states allow oral, or nuncupative, wills under specific conditions. For example, a California probate code states, in part, "A nuncupative will may be made by one who, at the time, is in actual military service in the field, or doing duty on shipboard at sea, and in either case in actual contemplation, fear, or peril of death, or by one who, at the time, is in expectation of immediate death from an injury received the same day." When allowed, such wills generally can pass only personal property and must be witnessed by two individuals.

3. The signature of the testate

As you would suspect, the signing of a will ordinarily must be done by its maker. But what if a person is severely ill or illiterate, and thus not capable of signing his full name? Then the mere making of a mark, such as an "X", can suffice in some situations. A person other than the will's maker may sign in the presence of the maker, as long as the maker has so directed. Or, at his request, the testate's hand may be guided by another to aid in the signing.

As you would suspect, the signing of a will ordinarily must be done by its maker.

21

4. *Signatures of witnesses*

In order for a will to be valid, statutes provide that it must be signed by two or three competent witnesses in the presence of the maker. To assess the competency of a witness, various factors are considered: Is the witness capable of testifying as to the facts of the execution of the will? Is he or she able to testify regarding the mental capacity of the testate? Generally, the witnesses do not need to know the contents of the will, but of course they must be aware that what they are signing is a will.

Generally, the witnesses do not need to know the contents of the will.

Will Modification

George Hamilton executed a will on March 31, 1982. In it he included a provision to leave his art collection to a museum, $15,000 to a close friend, and his stamp collection to his son. Two years later, his art collection was destroyed by a fire. To change his will, would he need to create an entirely new will? No, thanks to a handy amendment. A separate amendment modifying parts of an existing will is called a codicil. A codicil may replace the will entirely, or it may alter one or more clauses in the will and leave the rest unchanged. George cannot simply cross out the clause concerning the art collection, however, because most states require that a codicil meet the requirements prescribed for the execution of a valid will.

Revocation of a Will

Stephanie Miller takes a lighter out of her pocket and purposely sets fire to her will. Bob

Jones tears his will in half. Angela Hubble writes the word "canceled" in big red letters across each page of her will. Jack Johnson crosses out each clause of his will with a pen. Rebecca Sureman, with casts on both hands, asks her friend Lisa to burn Rebecca's will in the presence of her husband, Mark.

Are all of these people crazy? No. Remember, a will is revocable, meaning it can be terminated. Believe it or not, all of these methods of destroying a will are legitimate. As a Pennsylvania statute states: "by being burnt, torn, canceled, obliterated, or destroyed, with the intent and for the purpose of revocation, by the testator himself or by another person in his presence and by his express direction" a will may be revoked.

If the will maker is divorced after creating a will, the provisions in favor of the maker's former spouse are usually revoked.

In addition, a will can be revoked by operation of law. For example, if the maker marries after drawing a will, it is revoked in some states by the law. Or, if the will maker is divorced after creating a will, the provisions in favor of the maker's former spouse are usually revoked.

Will Contests

A lawsuit that challenges the validity of an existing will is called a will contest. Most contests are unsuccessful. Only a person who qualifies may make an objection to the probate court and request that a will be rejected. This would include someone who stands to lose a share of the decedent's estate, such as a spouse, heir, or devisee of an earlier will. If successfully contested and declared invalid by the probate court, the estate passes according to intestate succession laws. In effect, the assets are distributed as if the decedent had left no will.

There are several grounds that the court will accept to contest a will. For example, John McGee wrote and signed his will, but the will is not witnessed. Thus, the will is not properly executed and may be contested. Perhaps John is mentally retarded and incapable of understanding the meaning of his actions. Maybe John is tricked by his niece into believing that his only other heir is dead so that John leaves his estate to the niece. Or, John's will may leave the same items to different persons. In all of these cases, the will may be subject to a contest.

The "Simple" Will

The most utilized method of formal estate planning is the simple will. A will directs the administration and disposition of assets subject to probate. It is effective only upon approval by the probate court after death. Thus, a will, in effect, is a letter addressed to a judge in probate court. The executor, or personal representative, named in it presents it to the court, normally through an attorney. The personal representative then has the responsibility of carrying out its directions.

The most utilized method of formal estate planning is the simple will.

Sounds simple, doesn't it? Well, it isn't. Probate normally is a time-consuming, costly process. Costly in the financial sense and, even more significantly, costly in the sense of emotional strain and stress placed on the family. Probate may also openly expose the estate's financial affairs to the public, resulting in loss of privacy.

Advantages to a Will

If you are like most people, you want to have a say in the distribution of your estate. An estate will be distributed according to the intestate succession laws when no will exists. Such laws generally do not take into consideration the financial status of the decedent's relatives.

For example, Harry and Eleanor are the only surviving heirs of their mother, Monica. Harry is financially well-off, while Eleanor is destitute. If Monica dies intestate (without a will), her estate will be divided equally between her two children. If Monica had a will, she could have left a larger gift to the destitute child, Eleanor, and a smaller gift to the wealthy Harry.

A will allows you, as the testator, to choose who will be the personal representative, or executor.

A will allows you, as the testator (testatrix for females), to choose who will be the personal representative, or executor. The personal representative can have special powers relating to the estate. These include the power to sell property, the authority to settle claims, and the right to distribute the residue of the estate.

With a will, your estate may benefit from certain tax advantages. A will may even diminish the transfer taxes levied against devisees (those who receive the gifts made in the will). With the aid of a skillful estate planning attorney, techniques that minimize the amount of death taxes payable upon your death can be utilized.

Another advantage of a will is its low establishment cost. A will drawn up by an attorney is relatively inexpensive. If you are considering writing a will of your own though, it is important to remember that it must comply with state laws or it will be of little or no value upon your death. Preprinted fill-in-the-blanks wills are not likely to suit your particular circumstances. Rather than a joint will, you and your spouse should have individual wills for more flexibility and potential tax savings. A joint will may not be changeable by the surviving spouse.

Property transferred by a will is subject to scrutiny by a probate court before it may pass to your heirs.

Drawbacks to a Will

Though a person who dies with a will benefits his heirs more than a person who dies without one, potential disadvantages to a will still remain. Property transferred by a will is subject to scrutiny by a probate court before it may pass to your heirs. This time-consuming, expensive process often causes the most inconvenience to those whom you intended to benefit: your heirs.

DISADVANTAGES OF A WILL

- Requires Probate
- More expensive for heirs
- Significant time delays

Techniques for Distribution to Children

There are two main techniques for leaving assets to your children: per capita and per stirpes. Under per capita, each beneficiary receives the same amount. For example, suppose you have three children and one dies before you do, leaving three children of his own. You now have five beneficiaries, each of whom would receive 20 percent. This is true, if you designate that distribution is to take place per capita.

"Per Capita" Method	
Your child	20%
Your child	20%
Three children of deceased child (your grandchildren)	20% each

Suppose you designate distribution to be by the per stirpes method (which is synonymous with "by representation"). Then your assets would be divided into the number of equal shares that equals the number of your then surviving children. This would include any deceased child that leaves "issue" (children or grandchildren) then surviving. The share for each child is distributed to that child. The share of any deceased child leaving issue then surviving (your grandchildren, for example) is divided and distributed equally to those issue.

"Per Stirpes" Method	
Your child	33%
Your child	33%
Three children of deceased child (your grandchildren)	11% each

Your will should explain how you want your funeral expenses, debts and estate taxes to be paid.

Additional Provisions in a Will

Among other things, your will should explain how you want your funeral expenses, debts and estate taxes to be paid. Part of your will directs how your assets will be handed down. While leaving assets to your surviving spouse is fairly simple, deciding how to leave assets to your children and grandchildren is a little more complicated.

To reduce confusion, there are several provisions your will can include. Specific gifts (bequests or devises) should be made in detail. After all the gifts are made, a residuary clause can be included. This provides that anything not specifically mentioned in your will goes to whom you desire. Guardians should be named if you have minor children. An executor, or personal representative, should be named to handle all the details in transferring your estate.

A will places minimal burden on you during your lifetime. In other words, a will is a simple means of estate planning. However, because of the probate costs upon your death, a will may prove to be more expensive in the long run. With certain events in your life, such as a birth of a child, a death of anyone named in your will, a move to a different state, or if your economic circumstances change, your will should be reviewed and may need to be amended with a codicil.

A will places minimal burden on you during your lifetime.

Some people tend to minimize the time, effort and analysis needed in the preparation of a will. As a result, the heirs are often left with a disorganized estate that is time-consuming and expensive to settle. Disagreements may arise among those involved after your death. Generally, the advantages of a will adhere to you (due to the simplicity during your lifetime) and the disadvantages adhere to your heirs (due to potential problems and complications after your death).

SUMMARY

- A will does not avoid probate but is effective only if there are assets subject to probate and a court accepts it for probate.

- A will has a relatively low establishment cost.

- A will places minimal burden on you during your lifetime.

- A will may prove to be more expensive in the long run.

- The advantages of a will generally are yours while the disadvantages generally are your heirs.

CHAPTER SIX:
IS IS TRUST-WORTHY?
....

DEFINITIONS

Trustor(s) - The creator(s) of the trust.

Trustee(s) - The manager(s) of the trust who handles administration and distribution procedures according to the instructions of the trust.

Successor trustee(s) - The replacement of a trustee who stops being a trustee.

Institutional trustee - An institution, such as a trust department of a bank, that manages the administration procedures of the trust estate.

Beneficiaries - Persons for whom the trust was created.

Guardian - A person who has the legal right and duty to take care of another person, such as a child, who cannot legally take care of him- or herself.

The Origin of the Trust

Trusts first came into existence hundreds of years ago in England. Nobles were required to leave their land to their oldest male heirs, a system known as primogeniture. In order to gain control over their wealth transfer, nobles created the trust. Land was sold while a noble was still alive, but the buyer held it on behalf of another, usually the seller's heirs. Upon the noble's death, the land was not subject to primogeniture because he did not own the land.

> *In order to gain control over their wealth transfer, nobles created the trust.*

Trusts still exist today as a legal fiction created to hold assets. For example, they may hold assets for minors or incompetent adults. Or they may be used to hold and distribute assets in such a way as to reduce income or estate taxes. A "revocable" trust is normally one that can be revoked (voided) at any time and an "irrevocable" trust is one that cannot be revoked after it is executed. A "living" trust can be either revocable or irrevocable and is placed into existence by the trustor during the trustor's lifetime. Assets in the living trust avoid probate.

Testamentary Trust

A testamentary trust is established by the terms of your will. Thus, you must die before the trust goes into effect. None of your assets are actually placed in the trust during your lifetime. They normally must go through probate upon your death before they are placed in the trust. Unfortunately, the costs to your family may not end with the original probate expenses. There may be ongoing administrative costs for accounts and reports due to the court. Any investments and expenditures made with the testamentary trust may require petitions to the court for approval. The frequency with which these are due vary with each jurisdiction. Permission from the court may be required for investments, as well as various expenditures. Thus, the testamentary trust system can be burdensome. However, in most jurisdictions, there is little, if any, involvement with the court after probate administration is complete and the testamentary trust is established. That is assuming that the testamentary trust is properly written within the will.

Your assets normally must go through probate upon your death before they are placed in the trust.

If you are concerned about maintaining the privacy of your estate, a testamentary trust may not be for you. The testamentary trust is open to the public for review during the initial estate settlement phase. Any subsequent transaction that needs to be approved by the court is also open to the public. Such transactions include various investment activities, income generated from the trust, purchases, sales and other activities related to the trust estate.

The testamentary trust is open to the public for review during the initial estate settlement phase.

In the use of a testamentary trust, there may be a probate only on the first spouse's death. Suppose assets that were acquired by the second spouse were not properly transferred into the testamentary trust. Then a second probate upon the death of the second spouse may occur.

Living Trust

Perhaps you have attended a seminar on living trusts. "Living trusts are the best way to avoid probate," you were told. "Everybody needs one. Just sign here and our staff will prepare one for you for only a small amount!"

Just what is a living trust and why does everyone seem to be talking about it? Is it really that much better than other trust systems? Is it best for my particular circumstances? Furthermore, if I do decide on a living trust, who can best prepare one for me?

The living trust may also be called a revocable living trust, inter vivos (Latin for "while living") trust, A-B trust, or the double trust system. It is named the "living" trust because, unlike the testamentary trust, which does not go into effect until you die, the living trust is in effect during your lifetime. The living trust enables you to observe and control the trust, giving you the opportunity to alter or amend any provisions. This type of control is not possible with a will or an irrevocable trust. Remember that the living trust is a creature that is entirely dependent upon the words within it. Thus, it needs to be carefully drafted to contain the things that you want and which are appropriate to you.

The living trust is in effect during your lifetime.

From a legal point of view, having a living trust means that, since all your assets are inside the trust, you do not hold title to anything. Although you have relinquished ownership of your assets, if the trust is properly drafted you should retain control of those assets. This means you should have the power to buy, sell, transfer, borrow, or do whatever you wish with your assets. Since you have nothing in title in your own name, there is nothing to probate upon your death.

A living trust operates only on assets placed within it. Any asset you want placed within it must be retitled in the name of the trustees of the trust. If John and Mary Doe are the trustees, the title should read, "John and Mary Doe, or their successor trustees, as trustees of the John and Mary Doe Living trust dated _____, 199__." This is a long title and your banker or stockbroker may abbreviate it, but its gist needs to be present. Any assets purposely or inadvertently left out may have to go through probate. To simplify the trust, specific assets should not be named within its terminology. Otherwise an amendment might be necessary when the named asset is transferred out of the trust. Rather, the

Any assets purposely or inadvertently left out of the living trust may have to go through probate.

title document (the stock certificate, deed to your home, titlecard of your bank account, title certificate to your car, etc.) needs to be retitled in the name of your trust.

Is a "Schedule A" Necessary?

Many living trusts have a "Schedule A" or "Exhibit A" attached to it that is supposed to name the assets placed in the trust. While the idea may be good, this schedule is not necessary and often complicates matters. Seldom is it complete (it is often lost). It adds another piece of paper. Most importantly, naming the asset on the schedule does not retitle it and transfer it into the trust (as many people think it does). To be sure that an asset is transferred into the trust, its title document must be rewritten to name the trust.

Insurance Policies and Retirement Plans

There may be tax advantages in keeping your spouse as the first beneficiary and naming the trust as the second.

What about insurance policies and retirement plans? Each of these normally has a named beneficiary. If death occurs, the insurance proceeds or retirement funds are distributed to that beneficiary. They do not have to go through probate. Thus, it is normally not necessary to change ownership of these assets to the trust. You may want to change the beneficiary to be the trust, however. But be careful with any change of the beneficiary of a retirement plan. There may be tax advantages in keeping your spouse as the first beneficiary and naming the trust as the second, or contingent, beneficiary in the event your spouse does not survive you.

Living Trust Advantages

There are several advantages to the living trust form of estate planning: 1) it speeds up the distribution of your assets; 2) unlike a will or testamentary trust, normally no one may contest your wishes regarding the disposition of your estate; 3) the assets within the trust and their administration and distribution are not open to public review or scrutiny; 4) the living trust is totally revocable, meaning it may be changed at any time; and 5) its assets avoid the time and expense of probate, which is one of the primary advantages of the living trust. In fact, court interference can be avoided altogether. Thus, the administrative process is less expensive for the heirs, and the lengthy delays often associated with probate are eliminated.

ADVANTAGES TO A LIVING TRUST

- Avoid probate court interference
- Less expensive for heirs
- Lengthy delays eliminated

Suppose your aunt, Griping Gertrude, decides she deserves your mink coat, rather than Sweet Susie, whom you have named in your trust. After all, she sacrificed all those Sunday afternoons babysitting little Billie, didn't she? Griping Gertrude sets out to contest your living trust. It will not be as easy as she thinks, however. In contrast to a will, to contest a trust, Gertrude is required to hire a lawyer and file a civil suit. If your living trust is properly drafted, its assets are not frozen upon your death. This means the trustee can distribute them to the beneficiaries immediately. Gertie would then

In contrast to a will, to contest a trust, you are required to hire a lawyer and file a civil suit.

have to also sue each beneficiary. If your living trust has been in existence and use for a good while, it will be very difficult to successfully challenge it. Most likely, Griping Gertrude would have to go home, tail between her legs, in defeat.

Potential Living Trust Disadvantages

Potential disadvantages to the living trust include the establishment cost, typically from $700-1800 when a lawyer is involved. This is more than the cost of a will due to the additional time in drafting, explanation and assistance by an attorney. Assets that are to be transferred into the trust require retitling of their title documents in the name of the trust. You must also accept the responsibility of maintaining the trust. This is a necessary nuisance. You should be able to take care of this paperwork and the staff of your qualified attorney should be able to assist you if you need help.

LIVING TRUST DISADVANTAGES
- Establishment cost
- Nuisance factor
- Possible mismanagement

However, once the living trust is established and your assets are retitled in its name, maintenance should be simple. If you are a trustee and you control the trust, a separate income tax number is not necessary. You do not need to file a separate income tax return unless the trust becomes irrevocable. As you obtain additional assets, you simply title them in the name of your trust. When you sell an asset that is in the trust or transfer it out of the trust, you, as the trustee, simply sign the document that makes the transfer. Sometimes the buyer or transferee will want to see evidence of the existence of the trust to be sure you have authority to sell or transfer the asset. This is normally done by showing him a simple certificate of trust, a few pages of the trust, or the whole trust, if you do not mind. The only time you should need to see an attorney after the trust is established and funded is when you want to amend it.

Since you have removed the court from the administrative process, there exists the possibility of mismanagement by your successor trustee(s). So if your spouse subscribes to the old adage, "How can I be out of money, I still have checks?", your son thinks an "asset" is a type of chair, and your only other relative, Cousin Willie, spends most of his time in an igloo with Yamtuk and Eglo in Alaska, i.e., there are no individuals that you consider trustworthy enough to appoint as successor trustees, what are you to do? The trust department of a bank or other institution may be an appropriate alternative as successor trustee.

The trust department of a bank or other institution may be an appropriate alternative as successor trustee.

If your estate has serious creditor problems, the living trust may not be the best plan for you. The reason: your creditors may not be cut off as quickly as under probate. Under probate codes, there is a statutory period in which notice to creditors must be given. Typically, a creditor has four months after the first publication of notice to creditors in a local newspaper to file a claim against the probate estate. However, if you know about the creditor, you must notify him about the death and probate administration.

If your estate has serious creditor problems, the living trust may not be the best plan for you.

This must be done before his time period to file a claim begins running.

You may still use the living trust and not transfer all of your assets into it. Some assets would then be probated, causing the four month claim period to begin running. Generally, assets in a living trust are subject to a claims period for a specific period of time. Depending on the jurisdiction, this is often three years from the date of death of the trustor.

Although a living trust saves probate costs, it may not reduce estate or income taxes. Assets held in your living trust are still considered to be in your taxable estate. If the trust is properly written, estate and income taxes may be reduced after the death of a subsequent beneficiary, such as your spouse. Other techniques to reduce taxes, such as gifting, may also be utilized.

Establishing a Living Trust

There are two basic steps to the establishment of a living trust: 1) the creation of the physical document and 2) the transfer of property out of your name as an individual and into your name as a trustee.

Living Trust Two-Step Process:

1. CREATION

The trustors (trust creators) and the trustees (trust managers) are usually the same individuals when the trust is created.

Successor Trustee

The successor trustee takes over trust management upon the death, disability or resignation of the initial trustee. This transition takes place without requiring any court proceedings or legal action. To make the transition between the initial and successor trustee easy, proper drafting of the trust is very important. The successor trustee immediately has the same powers to buy, sell, borrow against, and transfer the trust assets. The successor trustee may not change the trust in any way, however. He or she must manage the assets in a prudent manner ("prudent" means the trustee cannot "invest" the trust assets at Saks Fifth Avenue). Suppose there is more than one successor trustee appointed. Then the trust should state whether a majority or all of the trustees must vote to make any decision.

The successor trustee takes over trust management upon the death, disability or resignation of the initial trustee.

The initial or successor trustee may be an individual, a number of individuals, an institution (a trust department of a bank, for example) or a combination of these. If an institutional trustee is appointed, the family does not have the responsibilities of daily management of trust assets. Assuming the trust is properly prepared, an individual trustee could delegate administration duties and investment management to someone else, such as a bank or private company. Naming a trust department in a bank as the successor trustee has its advantages. For example, there will be someone with a deep pocket that is accountable in case problems arise. A trust institution may be helpful if you simply do not want to manage your own assets.

Trust Beneficiaries

The beneficiaries, or persons for whose benefit a trust is created, are usually the same individuals as the trustors as long as they are alive. If you are married, your surviving spouse would most likely be the primary beneficiary as well as the surviving trustee after your death. Your children and other named heirs may be the contingent beneficiaries. This means they would be beneficiaries only if they are living when your surviving spouse dies. Of course, there must be assets left in the trust for distribution to them.

Pourover Will

A "pourover" will may be necessary to transfer assets inadvertently left out of your trust. An executor (or "personal representative" in some jurisdictions) should be named in your will to administrate such assets. Upon your death, the executor takes these assets through probate and then "pours" them into the trust. For practical purposes, it is advisable to name an executor residing in the state where the probate takes place. In addition, a guardian should be named for minor children and handicapped individuals.

2. TRANSFER PROCESS

To completely avoid the probate process, all of your assets must be placed in the living trust. The title to your home, bank accounts, stocks, and all other major assets of your estate must be changed so the records reflect a transfer into the trust has been made. Though this will involve paperwork and time, it is an important process.

You can do much of the paperwork yourself, particularly if your attorney gives you written instructions. Remember, even though your assets are held in trust, you still may sell or add new assets to the trust and maintain complete control. Once again, this is assuming your trust is properly prepared. As trustee, you make the decisions, and you will not have to pay anyone a trust management fee.

EXAMPLES, TRANSFER PROCESS

From : Mr. & Mrs. Smith as joint tenants To : Mr. & Mrs. Smith as trustees
From : Ms Jones, a single person To : Ms Jones, as trustee

SUMMARY

- A person must die before a testamentary trust goes into effect.

- With a testamentary trust, assets usually must go through probate.

- The living trust is in effect during your lifetime.

- You maintain control of your assets with a living trust.

- Properly drafted and funded, a living trust avoids probate.

- A living trust is one of the most private means of distribution.

- A living trust should be totally revocable.

- You should transfer your assets into your living trust.

- You have the option of appointing an institutional trustee to help manage your estate.

- To be most effective and appropriate for you and your family situation, a trust must be carefully and properly drafted.

CHAPTER SEVEN:
WHAT YOU NEED TO KNOW ABOUT ESTATE TAXES

Your estate may be subject to two levels of taxation upon your death, one on the federal level and one on the state level. The federal level consists of estate taxes and generation-skipping taxes, and the state level has estate or inheritance taxes. Any taxes that have to be paid and any reports that have to be filed, normally are due nine months after the date of death. Without proper planning, such taxes can essentially destroy your estate, taking away up to half of your assets.

ESTATE TAX SYSTEM

In order for you to know how to minimize and even eliminate these taxes altogether, it is important for you to be knowledgeable of the federal and state estate tax systems. You should know when your estate is subject to these taxes and how much of your estate is affected. Any estate planning you do should provide appropriate means of having the needed liquidity (easily converted to cash) to pay taxes. This should be done without having to sell your major assets.

Without proper planning, taxes can essentially destroy your estate, taking away up to half of your assets.

State Tax

The approach of states to inheritance tax differs from the federal government. The federal government calculates by adding all asset values and subtracting legally allowed deductions and tax credits. State inheritance taxes are much more complex. Tax rates are based upon the class of the beneficiary: if the beneficiary is the spouse, the rate is much lower than for children. The children's rates are less than those applied to distant relatives, and when assets are left to strangers, the rate is considerably higher.

Today, very few states have inheritance taxes. Most inheritance taxes have been replaced by a "pick-up" tax which involves a much simpler calculation. This system simply picks up the credit that the federal system automatically allows for state tax. In other words, part of every estate tax dollar which would otherwise be payable to the federal government is diverted to the appropriate state government.

Beware of any state that advertises it does not have any estate tax.

Beware of any state that advertises it does not have any estate tax. Florida, Texas and Nevada sometimes advertise this. While it may be technically correct that an estate tax is not charged by that state, federal law dictates that the credit given for anticipated state estate taxes will have to be paid to the federal government if not used by the state!

Federal Tax

Under the current federal taxation system, if your net worth is less than $600,000 at the time of death, there is an exemption and no tax liability is incurred. Assuming the estate is properly planned, married persons can shelter up to $1.2 million. Tax on each additional dollar starts at 37% and goes up to 50% for estates of $2.5 million or more. From about $10,000,000 to $18,000,000 the tax rate is 55%, and then it drops back to 50%. Life insurance is included in this calculation.

FEDERAL ESTATE TAX

Net Estate	Taxable Estate	Tax
$ 700,000	$ 100,000	$ 37,000
800,000	200,000	75,000
900,000	300,000	133,500
1,000,000	400,000	153,000
1,200,000	600,000	235,000
1,500,000	900,000	363,000
2,000,000	1,400,000	658,000
3,000,000	2,400,000	1,650,000

Tax Reforms You Should Know About

Recently, there have been tax reforms that greatly influence estate planning.

Recently, there have been tax reforms that greatly influence estate planning. Of these, the three most significant include Unlimited Marital Deduction, Unified Credit, Maximum Federal Estate Taxes, and Generation Skipping Tax. As of the printing of this book other reforms are under federal review by Congress.

1. *Unlimited Marital Deduction (Maximum Marital Deduction)*

The Unlimited Marital Deduction enables a spouse to pass his or her entire estate to the other spouse free of gift or estate taxes. This frees the surviving spouse from having to liquidate lifetime assets in order to pay estate taxes. In other words, your spouse will not have to sell your home to pay the estate taxes when you die. Thanks to the Unlimited Marital Deduction, any asset of yours that goes to your spouse as a result of your death will not be subject to any federal estate tax.

Although it is of great benefit to the surviving spouse, using the Unlimited Marital Deduction may result in losing the benefits of unified credit.

2. Unified Credit (federal estate tax equivalent exemption)

It is termed a "credit" because each estate is potentially credited, or exempted, $192,800. This is the amount of estate tax that would be owed on an estate valued at $600,000. Each dollar over $600,000 is taxed beginning at 37%, and up to 50% for estates valued at $2.5 million or more. For a married couple, each spouse has an equivalent exemption of $600,000. Therefore, $1.2 million is the total exemption for a married couple. Many people lose this dual exemption due to poor estate planning.

Using the Unlimited Marital Deduction may result in losing the benefits of unified credit.

3. Maximum Federal Estate Taxes

The federal estate tax grows as your estate increases in size, beginning at 37% above $600,000 and topping out at 50% above $2,500,000. The 1981 tax code gradually reduced the maximum tax from 70% to 50%.

"My estate's only worth $300,000," you may be thinking. "With the federal estate tax equivalent exemption of $600,000, why would I need to do any estate tax planning?" Remember, however, that inflation will reduce the real benefit of the equivalent exemption. With an inflation rate of 7 percent per year, your $300,000 estate would increase to a worth of $600,000 in only ten years, or $1.2 million in 20 years.

4. Generation Skipping Tax

Many families with substantial estates have reduced estate taxes by skipping a generation.

Typically this is done by gifting directly to grandchildren or a more distant generation. Another tactic is to establish a trust whereby children are to receive limited lifetime benefits and then the remainder is to be distributed to a later generation (grandchildren, great-grandchildren, etc.). This way a generation is skipped that otherwise would be subject to estate tax upon the death of that generation member. However, this was limited in 1987 by an addition to federal tax law called "The Generation Skipping Tax". Generally speaking, each individual making such a gift, either during his lifetime or at his death, has an exemption of $1,000,000. Any amount over that is taxed at a flat 55% rate, and is due at the time of the death of the skipped person.

Many families with substantial estates have reduced estate taxes by skipping a generation.

SUMMARY

- There are two levels of estate taxes, state and federal.

- Inheritance tax is a state tax upon the right to inherit in an amount that is based upon the class of the beneficiary.

- Estate tax is a tax levied upon your estate when you die at the federal level, state level, or both.

- The "pick-up" tax diverts part of every dollar which would otherwise be transferred to the federal government to the appropriate state government.

- Life insurance is included in calculating the size of your estate.

- The unlimited marital deduction enables a spouse to pass his or her entire estate to

the other spouse free of gift or estate
taxes.

- With the federal estate tax equivalent
  exemption, each estate is exempted
  $192,800, or the amount of estate tax that
  would be owed on an estate valued at
  $600,000.

- The maximum federal estate tax is 50%
  and 55% for very large estates.

- The federal generation skipping tax has
  an exemption of $1,000,000 and is at a flat
  rate of 55%.

CHAPTER EIGHT:
UNDERSTANDING THE LIVING TRUST

Basic Forms of the Living Trust

There are three basic forms of a living trust: 1) the simple trust; 2) the A-B trust; and 3) the A-B-C trust. The names of these three forms are often different, but the concepts for each are the same. The form that is best for you depends upon a number of factors, including your marital status, the net worth of your estate, and the distribution you desire for your heirs.

1. Simple Trust

The simple trust is normally for a single person who has an estate of any size. Its provisions should be tailor-made for that individual's family, asset and tax situation. A husband and wife who are not concerned about estate taxes may also use the simple trust. If properly prepared, both spouses can use just one trust together. A trust for each is not necessary. The administration and distribution of a simple trust are just that: simple. The estate is not large enough to be subject to estate taxes, so estate tax reduction provisions are normally not included in the simple trust. The trust may continue on after death or distribute out and terminate. Many options are available.

> *The simple trust is normally for a single person who has an estate of any size.*

2. A-B Trust

When a married couple is involved in the trust and their combined estate may be taxable (remember the $600,000 exemption?) the A-B trust should be considered. The way it works is this: when one spouse dies, that spouse's share of the assets up to $600,000 would flow into the B (sometimes called the "decedent's" or "family") trust. The single trust is thus divided into two trusts (A and B) upon the death of the first spouse. The provisions in the B trust can be flexible and discretionary, but normally use of its assets by the surviving spouse is limited to that spouse's "health, education, support and maintenance." The surviving spouse's share and the remaining share of the deceased spouse, if any, is placed into the A, or survivor's, trust. The surviving spouse normally has complete control over the A trust.

Thus, upon the first death, there would not be any federal estate taxes because the federal estate tax exemption and marital deduction are fully utilized. And then, upon the death of the surviving spouse, whatever is inside the B trust, including any increase in value, is not taxable in that spouse's estate. Thus, both federal estate tax exemptions are utilized, resulting in considerable tax savings.

As long as the value of the combined estate remains below $1.2 million, or two federal estate tax equivalent exemptions, no estate tax is due. If only an A trust was used, when the surviving spouse dies every dollar in excess of $600,000 would be taxed, beginning at 37%. An A-B trust allows for substantial growth in the B trust without estate taxes. Any assets expected to appreciate in value could be placed in the B trust upon the death of the first spouse. This would insulate the growth from taxation in the estate of the surviving spouse upon that spouse's death,

As long as the value of the estate remains below $1.2 million, or two federal estate tax equivalent exemptions, no estate tax is due.

even though the surviving spouse has lifetime use of the B trust assets.

3. A-B-C Trust

This trust form is used for a married couple whose combined estate exceeds $1.2 million, or two federal estate tax equivalent exemptions. Upon the death of the first spouse, $600,000 of that spouse's share is distributed into the B trust, and any remaining assets of that spouse's share are distributed into the C trust, potentially preventing estate taxation. Any share that the surviving spouse has typically flows into the A trust.

Q-TIPS Clean Up

A Q-TIP (Qualified Terminable Interest Property) trust is most commonly used with a second marriage.

The C trust is also known as a Q-TIP (Qualified Terminable Interest Property) trust and is most commonly used with a second marriage. Take, for example, the situation Steve is in. He is a successful business owner in his late 60s and is now married to his second wife, Alicia. Both Steve and Alicia each have two children from their first marriages. Alicia is more than a dozen years younger than Steve, and only ten years older than Steve's oldest son, Bob. If he were to follow traditional estate planning, Steve would leave $600,000 to his children and $1.4 million to Alicia. When Alicia dies, she can leave that $1.4 million to her own children, leaving only the first $600,000 to Steve's children.

This situation can be avoided if Steve decides to use a Q-TIP. Instead of leaving the $1.4 million to Alicia, Steve specifies that these assets are put in a Q-TIP trust. Alicia must receive all the income from the $1.4 million as long as she lives. Upon her death, the trust funds go where Steve has directed them: to his children. In this way he is assured that his money will end up where he wants it.

The income from the property in the Q-TIP trust must be solely for the surviving spouse during his or her lifetime in order to qualify for the unlimited marital deduction. Even though the surviving spouse has no say in where the assets eventually will go, estate taxes will be deferred on assets placed in the Q-TIP until the surviving spouse's death.

Q-TIPS are not just popular in second marriages when each spouse has children from previous marriages. They can be beneficial if you are still married to your high school sweetheart. Suppose you have a massive heart attack and die tomorrow. Your spouse may eventually remarry and even start a second family or marry into one that is ready-made. The Q-TIP can provide lifetime income for your spouse. It will also make sure that your assets will find their way to your own children, rather than the children or stepchildren of your spouse's next marriage.

Q-TIPS can be beneficial if you are still married to your high school sweetheart.

Providing for Minor or Handicapped Children

If you have children or are planning to in the future, it is advisable to name a guardian of your choice and provide for your children's welfare through a trust. This assures you they will be well provided for in the event something were to happen to you as parents. If you neither have a living trust nor a will at the time of your death, the court will require that a guardianship and conservatorship be set up through the probate court until the minor children become adults or for the continuing care of the handicapped individuals. The court also will appoint a guardian and conservator who is required to regularly report to the court. The guardianship and conservatorship created by the court, in order to protect your assets and benefit your children, is by necessity very restrictive. A living trust enables you to provide for your children and/or grandchildren in the manner you desire, rather than having a court guess your personal desires for their care.

A living trust enables you to provide for your children and/or grandchildren in the manner **you** *desire.*

SUMMARY

- With an A-B trust, part of the deceased spouse's assets flow into the B trust.

- Properly prepared, an A-B trust uses federal estate tax exemptions of both spouses.

- With a Q-TIP trust, estate taxes can be deferred. Income must be used for the surviving spouse, and assets within it can go to your children after the death of the surviving spouse.

- It is advisable to name a guardian and conservator to provide for your children's welfare.

CHAPTER NINE:
OTHER DOCUMENTS

Pourover Wills

Because it specifically spells out to whom, when and how your assets are to be distributed, the living trust, in effect, becomes your will. However, the pourover will is needed to accompany the living trust. The pourover will transfers into the trust assets that have been purposely or inadvertently left outside. In effect, it says that if you do not retitle an asset into your living trust, it is your intent that it be placed into your trust when you die. The probate process is then initiated, and the will is proved for probate. The asset is then "poured over" into your living trust through probate administration and the distribution provisions in your will.

> *The pourover will transfers into the trust assets that have been purposely or inadvertently left outside.*

A pourover will normally consists of five provisions: 1) it identifies the individual by name; 2) it revokes any prior wills and codicils; 3) it pours into the living trust any personal or household effects left outside the trust; 4) it pours into the trust any real assets left outside the trust (after probate); and 5) it names the executor and provides the necessary authority to take assets left outside the trust through probate. If you have minor children, it should also name a guardian and conservator for them.

A document entitled Personal Property Memorandum may be used to transfer personal and household effects either into the trust or to named individuals. If such things are not taken care of in this way, the pourover will restates that they are to pour over into the living trust.

The pourover will also specifies that any other assets subject to probate are to pour over into the trust upon your death. This may include checking accounts, savings accounts, money market funds, certificates of deposit, treasury bills, stocks, bonds, mutual funds, limited partnerships, notes due to you, real estate, trust deeds, and business interests. Remember that assets held in joint tenancy are neither in the trust nor affected by the will. They simply pass to the surviving joint tenant.

Typically the surviving spouse is named in the pourover will as the executor. Upon the death of the surviving spouse, the successor trustee should be named to serve as the executor. The pourover will provides the executor with the authority to take any assets left outside the trust through the probate process. Once this is completed, the assets pour over into your living trust.

Other Uses for the Pourover Will

Along with pouring into the trust assets inadvertently left out, there are two other potential uses for the pourover will. Suppose you were killed by a drunk driver in an automobile accident. Your family sues the drunk driver and is awarded $100,000 in a wrongful death suit. Such proceeds would become a part of your estate. Thanks to the pourover will, the $100,000 would pour over into your living trust.

Individuals with substantial assets who are concerned about potential exposure to liability suits can also make good use of the pourover will. In today's sue-crazy society, the possibility of a lawsuit, regardless of its merits, certainly exists. If a lawsuit were to go through the overcrowded civil courts, it could take many years to resolve. The cost in legal fees could be a very significant amount. The probate court, on the other hand, may hear the claim much sooner and may be inclined to discharge the claim. With a civil trial, the emotional whims of a jury may take part in settling a case, whereas the probate court is more likely to settle it on the basis of the true merits of the claim. Therefore, it may be more beneficial to have such claims heard in the probate court. Once the claims have been settled, the remaining assets can then be distributed into the trust to be used as specified.

Living Will

Probably the last thing you can (or want to) imagine right now is lying in a hospital bed, hooked up to a respirator, sustained by a feeding tube. But medical science has progressed to the point where we can be kept alive long after we are getting anything out of life. In the event you or your spouse are in a terminally ill condition, your family must address such issues as what limitations will be imposed on efforts to revive or resuscitate. The overriding consideration in such difficult decisions should be "What would the patient want done?" Unfortunately, the patient is often unconscious or otherwise incompetent to make informed personal decisions.

The living will is designed to allow you to specify in advance what treatment you would desire if you have no hope of surviving.

Is there a solution? The living will is designed to allow you to specify in advance what treatment you would desire if you have no hope of surviving. Hence, the living will is becoming more important as a part of estate planning. Many millions of people in the United States have drawn up living wills. The living will states, in effect, that if your life is being sustained solely by artificial means, you want the life support disconnected. Of course, this decision must be made while you are competent. Such a living will might read:

> **"If I should have an incurable or irreversible condition that will cause my death within a relatively short time, it is my desire that my life not be prolonged by administration of life-sustaining procedures. If my condition is terminal and I am unable to participate in decisions regarding my medical treatment, I direct my attending physician to withhold or withdraw procedures that merely prolong the dying process and are not necessary to my comfort or freedom from pain."**

Living wills may even specify what sort of therapies you do or do not want applied in a terminal situation. The clearer and more convincing you are in making your wishes known, the greater the chance they will be upheld. That is why you should be as specific as possible in drawing up your living will. For example, you could state that if you have an incurable disease or an irreversible physical or mental condition with no recovery in sight, you do not want medical treatment. Or you might specify that if you are permanently unconscious, you want to be treated with pain-killing drugs but no cardiac resuscitation or mechanical respiration.

Living wills are now recognized in nearly all states. The courts and the medical professions have slowly come to the realization that each

The clearer and more convincing you are in making your wishes known, the greater the chance they will be upheld.

person does have a right to decide about his or her quality of life. Recent court decisions have begun to uphold an individual's right to die.

On the night of January 11, 1983, Nancy Cruzan lost control of her car as she traveled down Elm Road in Jasper County, Missouri. The vehicle overturned, and Nancy was discovered lying face down in a ditch without detectable respiratory or cardiac function. It was estimated that Nancy was deprived of oxygen from 12 to 14 minutes. Permanent brain damage generally results after 6 minutes of oxygen deprivation. Nancy remained in a coma for approximately three weeks. She then progressed to an unconscious state in which she was able to orally ingest some nutrition. Nancy remained in this state for about eight years until she died. She was oblivious to her surroundings and her body twitched only reflexively, without consciousness. Because Nancy could not swallow, her nutrition and hydration were delivered through a tube surgically implanted in her stomach.

Nancy's parents, husband and friends fought with the courts to have Nancy's nutrition and hydration terminated. Nancy's former roommate even quoted her as saying, at age 25, that "if sick or injured she would not wish to continue her life unless she could live at least halfway normally." However, the Missouri Supreme Court held that since there was not "clear and convincing evidence of the incompetent's wishes to the withdrawal of life-sustaining treatment", the family's wishes would not be carried out. The United States Supreme Court agreed. This turmoil would have been avoided if Nancy had a living will.

The courts and the medical professions have slowly come to the realization that each person does have a right to decide about his or her quality of life.

Another widely reported case involved Karen Ann Quinlan. Karen lapsed into a coma after ingesting a mixture of alcohol and barbiturates at a party. For about a year, Karen's parents fought with the court to have their daughter removed from a respirator. In 1975, the New Jersey Supreme court ruled unanimously in favor of the Quinlans, and Karen was removed from the respirator. Amazingly, Karen continued to live another nine years. Karen's was a case that began a process that has made the medical and legal professions aware of an individual's right to determine his or her quality of life.

A living will effectively removes the burden of a "let live" or "let die" decision from your family.

A living will effectively removes the burden of a "let live" or "let die" decision from your family and doctor. It removes the financial strain as well. Although you may be fully covered by Medicare or private health insurance, it is more likely that part of your assets will be diverted to the health-care industry. Someone has to pay for all the doctors, nurses, and high-tech machinery.

Even with a living will, the results you desire may not be achieved. Some doctors simply will not make life-or-death decisions on the basis of a piece of paper. That is why it is advisable to supplement your living will with a medical power of attorney.

Nearly all states now have a statutory form for a living will. Unfortunately, there is not much uniformity from state to state. You should have a living will that closely or verbatim follows the statutory form of the state where you reside. Remember that the laws in this area continue to change from state to state so that you should periodically update your living will. And, should you be in a different state when the catastrophe occurs, your living will could be enforced with a medical power of attorney.

Medical Power of Attorney

You should have a living will that closely or verbatim follows the statutory form of the state where you reside.

The primary purpose of a medical power of attorney is to appoint someone to make health care decisions in the event you are unable to. Only one attorney-in-fact (usually your spouse) should be appointed to avoid a tug-of-war over your body. An alternate attorney-in-fact (such as an adult child, other family member, or close friend) can be named in the event something were to happen to the original attorney-in-fact. Because doctors and hospitals have less to fear from liability suits, it is most likely that your attorney-in-fact's wishes will be followed.

Suppose you are involved in an automobile accident. You are rushed to the hospital, unconscious, and surgery is necessary. In this situation, the hospital and the doctors would need an authorization to perform such surgery. Contrary to common assumption, your children do not have the power to authorize the doctor or hospital to perform surgery or life-saving acts on your behalf. In fact, parents cannot even authorize emergency treatment for their legally adult children. But the authorization needed can be provided by a person who legally holds your medical power of attorney (your attorney-in-fact).

In most emergency situations, the spouse would have the right to sign any medical release if the other spouse is incompetent. Normally, the conscious spouse would not be required to provide a medical power of attorney. But there may be a time when its use is needed by the other spouse. What if the other spouse is not available or doesn't even exist? The medical power of attorney is there to designate and empower another individual to assist you and carry out your wishes.

Durable Power of Attorney

The durable power of attorney can deal with many things.

While the medical power of attorney is limited to health care things, the durable power of attorney can deal with many things. It is "durable" if it contains the words "this power of attorney survives any disability of mine" or similar words. Without this phrase, the law dictates that it will automatically terminate upon your incompetency, just when you need it the most!

In your durable power of attorney, you designate an agent to act upon your behalf to do the things listed in it. It either goes into effect when you sign it or springs into effect when you become incompetent, depending upon what you choose. It can allow your agent to sign a deed for your home, deal with a nursing home, the IRS or Social Security, or transfer assets into your living trust if you have one.

Without the power of attorney, if you become incompetent or disappear, it will be necessary to go to court to have someone appointed to do these things for you. This involves the appointment of a guardian (to take care of your person) or conservator (to take care of your assets and business things), or both. It normally requires two attorneys (one for the petitioner and one to represent you), at least one doctor, and someone appointed by the court to look at everything. This process is often time consuming, expensive, and traumatic to the family as well as to you. If you have a living trust, the assets inside it are protected from this.

Competency Clause in Living Trust or Power of Attorney

Consider the situation of poor old Betty Limerick. A widow for the past nine years, Betty had acquired a sizable estate when her husband Lloyd passed away. Following Lloyd's death, Betty had made some wise investments, doubling the size of her assets. Although her daughter had attempted to talk Betty into establishing a living trust, Betty refused to do so. Joseph Bland, a rather unscrupulous attorney, became aware of Betty's situation. Mr. Bland made a request of the court that he gain control of Betty's assets, stating she "has been making poor investments, has been losing money, and in order to preserve her assets, I ask that I be appointed her conservator." Joseph Bland's request was granted, and Betty lost control of all her funds. Steps were taken in the courts to have control returned to Betty. The process took over six months and incurred substantial legal costs, not to mention the fees extracted by Mr. Joseph Bland, Esq.

The legal process is much simpler if the competency clause is utilized.

Unfortunately, such occurrences are not unheard of. There are many people out there just waiting to exploit elderly and often infirm individuals. What can be done to avoid a situation such as Betty Limerick's? If you have a living trust and you are a trustee, the trust should contain a competency provision that defines when someone should take over for you. Assets within the trust are controlled by the trust's provisions and are not subjected to any court process. The competency provision within the trust should provide for the smooth transition of the successor trustee, or simply your spouse as the other trustee, to take over for you.

If you do not have a living trust but have a durable power of attorney that is effective now (that is, it does not "spring" into effect upon your incompetency but can be used right away), the agent that you appoint could do the things that Joseph Bland had to go to court to gain permission to do. And if it were a springing power of attorney, the competency clause within it would define when your agent would take over for you and have the power to do the things needed.

The competency provision, whether it is in your living trust or springing power of attorney, should focus on a medical determination. One, or preferably two doctors should be required to make a written statement that you are no longer able to manage your affairs. These statements are then attached to your living trust or springing power of attorney.

Appointing a Conservator and Guardian

As you can see, the competency clause authorizes your successor trustee to administer your assets. Another document, the appointment of conservator and guardian, identifies whom you want to be responsible for your person if you become incompetent. Basically, your guardian would care for your physical needs, while your conservator takes care of financial matters. If you so desire, the guardian and conservator may be the same person. In other words, the conservator and guardian becomes responsible for ensuring your safety and well-being. Rather than the court appointing someone for you, this provision enables you to name someone you trust. If you were to come down with Alzheimer's disease or some other malady, your guardian would help provide you with the finest care possible, and your conservator would manage your financial matters.

Personal Property Memorandum

We have noted earlier the importance of transferring all of your assets into the living trust, thus avoiding probate. For items that have a written title document, the title is simply rewritten to reflect that it has been transferred into the trust. But what is done with assets that have no written title; that is, personal and household effects, such as furniture, appliances, furnishings, pictures, china, silverware, glass, books, jewelry, clothing, etc.? A separate document entitled "Personal Property Memorandum" transfers such items into the trust. Or, the trust itself can include a provision that transfers all such property to the trust merely by executing the trust. The process is completed without a detailed inventory. The Personal Property Memorandum might also be used to accompany the will or trust to independently designate distribution of the items named within upon your death.

Anatomical Gift

We are all familiar with the little box on our driver's license that we either checked or left blank next to "organ donor." Many consider it noble to gift their vital organs upon their death to help save lives or to provide sight to elderly people with glaucoma. However, rather than stating your desire on the back of your driver's license for all to see, it has been recommended that you use a separate legal document to be incorporated with your estate plan. Think about it: If you were in that gray area between life and death, would you want your doctor to take those vital organs prematurely?

Separate Property Agreement

As you will recall, separate property is defined as property received by one spouse as a gift or inheritance, or property obtained prior to marriage. Suppose, after ten years of marriage, you receive $10,000 in stock when your Uncle Jimmy dies. You later decide to use the money to put a swimming pool in your backyard. Before you know it, this asset has become a part of the marriage property as a whole. The money from the stock has lost its identity as separate property. In situations such as this, what can be done so such assets retain their characteristic as separate property? A separate property agreement can be utilized. This document lists the separate property of each spouse and is attached to your living trust. The assets separately belonging to each spouse are brought together for the enjoyment of both spouses. When the surviving spouse dies, the separate property will go to the heirs specified by the spouse who owned the property.

When a husband and wife have each been married before and both have children by their former marriages, a separate property agreement can be useful. Upon the death of one of them, the surviving spouse can continue to enjoy the standard of living he or she is accustomed to. When the surviving spouse dies, however, each spouse most likely wants his or her share of the estate to pass to the children of his or her former marriage. A separate property agreement is a means toward that end.

When a husband and wife both have children by their former marriages, a separate property agreement can be useful.

SUMMARY

- The pourover will transfers assets left out of your living trust into the trust.

- The living will allows you to specify in advance what treatment you would desire in your last days.

- Your living will should comply with the statutory form of the state where you reside.

- The primary purpose of a medical power of attorney is to appoint someone to make health care decisions in the event you are unable to.

- The durable power of attorney permits your agent to do the things designated within it.

- With a competency clause, if you become incompetent, your successor trustee could take over for you.

- A guardian is responsible for your person if you become incompetent, and a conservator for your financial matters.

- The personal property memorandum transfers items with no written title into the trust or to named individuals.

- A separate property agreement lists the separate property of each spouse and can be attached to your living trust.

CHAPTER TEN:
TAXED TO THE MAX? WHAT CAN HELP ....

Gifting

For tax-saving purposes, there are two types of gifts available under current law:

1. $10,000 gift per person per year

2. $600,000 gift in a lifetime

The $10,000 gift provision allows you to gift up to $10,000 per person per year, without being subject to gift or estate taxes, to as many individuals as you desire. If you are married, you and your spouse can give up to $20,000 per donee, per year.

> The $10,000 gift provision allows you to gift $10,000 per person per year, without being subject to gift or estate taxes.

If you pay someone else's medical bills or school tuition directly, these payments are not counted toward the $10,000 limit. Most people choose to use this provision with their children and/or grandchildren. Federal Gift Tax Form 709 must be filed on April 15 of each year if any gift exceeds $10,000.

Under current law, the person receiving the gift must acquire a "present interest" in that gift in order that the $10,000 gift exclusion be allowed. However, recent tax decisions have held that if the money is given to a person from a living trust, the person receiving the gift is not getting a "present interest." Currently before Congress is an act that, if it passes, would mean that any gift from a properly prepared revocable living trust will be considered a present interest, so that it will qualify for the $10,000 annual exclusion.

The one-time lifetime gift of $600,000 allows you to gift $600,000 to the individual of your choice. Or, up to $1.2 million may be gifted, with proper estate planning, if you are married. However, any money gifted above this amount is subject to taxation, the gift tax being the same as the estate tax. In determining the value of your estate, any gifts (aside from the $10,000 exclusion) that have been made from your estate since December 31, 1976, are added by the IRS back into your estate. Thus, gifting in this form does not reduce your estate for estate tax purposes. By using part or all of the $600,000 exemption in lifetime gifts, you also use and reduce in like amounts the $600,000 exemption that is otherwise available to your estate upon your death.

Since the federal government has been running huge budget deficits for years, tax increases will likely be enacted to close that deficit. The estate and gift tax is a possible target. You should keep abreast of these changes in order to have your trust or will appropriately adjusted.

If you decide to use these gift exemptions, what can you give? Although cash gifts are the simplest, you may want to give away assets that are likely to appreciate, such as real estate or portfolios of stocks or mutual funds. This removes any future appreciation from your estate. For example, suppose you own a vacation home in Vail. Getting up in years, you and your wife no longer ski and rarely use the home. When the market peaked a number of years ago, the home had a value of $400,000. Currently, the house is appraised at $300,000. So you decide to give the house to your children, using the annual exclusion and part of your gift tax exemption. If the market rises as expected, and the home value increases back to $400,000, that appreciation is out of your estate, as well as the asset itself.

Insurance Trust

Of all the estate tax revenues that the IRS collects, insurance policies are the biggest source. Ninety percent of all life insurance policies are reportedly held in such a way that they are vulnerable to estate tax. Usually, life insurance proceeds are exempt from income tax. It is the estate tax that you need to be concerned with.

Usually, life insurance proceeds are exempt from income tax. It is the estate tax that you need be concerned with.

Is there a way to remove your policies from your estate to avoid taxation? The answer could lie in changing the ownership of the life insurance policy so it is not included in your estate when you die. The insurance proceeds would then be tax-free. By applying for a policy on your life and paying the premiums, your children could own the policy. They would be named the beneficiaries so they would collect the proceeds at your death. If the premiums are too expensive, you can make cash gifts to provide them with enough money.

Problems may arise with this method, however. Life insurance policies often have a cash value of up to hundreds of thousands of dollars. If the children own the policy, it may be too easy for them to take money out by means of loans or withdrawals. Then, when the money is needed, it will not be there. Even if you trust your children absolutely, there still remains a chance they will get into a divorce fight sometime in the future. Since an insurance policy held by one spouse becomes a marital asset, your son-or daughter-in-law may demand half the value.

Additionally, the policy may be seized if one of your children is involved in an accident and held liable for damages. Or there could be a business failure, with creditors demanding to be paid off. In either situation, the policy would not be available for paying estate tax.

Is there a solution? The insurance trust enables you to place a life insurance policy inside the insurance trust without any gift tax consequences. You cannot be the trustee, but your child or children can be named as trustees. Upon your death, the insurance company will pay the face value of the insurance policy to them. In this way your children, as trustees, can have effective control over the assets of the trust (the insurance policy) without the risks of direct ownership. Even though it is irrevocable, you effectively still maintain control over the insurance trust. How? As soon as you cease making gifts to the trust to pay the policy premiums, the insurance company will reduce or cancel the policy.

The insurance trust is beneficial for estate tax saving purposes.

The insurance trust is beneficial for estate tax saving purposes. Funds paid by the insurance company upon your death are, in effect, removed from your estate. Your insurance policies, as you will recall, are typically included when your estate's worth is calculated for estate tax purposes. Since the insurance trust is considered the owner and the beneficiary of the insurance, however, your policies are not counted as part of your estate. Yet, the trustees may still use these insurance funds to provide for your surviving spouse, your children, and to pay estate taxes.

For individuals with large estates, the least expensive way to pay taxes may be with insurance. Primarily, insurance provides liquidity. Since the assets of most people's estates cannot readily be converted into cash, their estates are seldom liquid. This means the assets of the estate are often sold for less than their actual worth, due to the fact they had to be sold quickly to obtain cash for estate taxes. In contrast, insurance could provide such cash liquidity.

For individuals with large estates, the least expensive way to pay taxes may be with insurance.

Failure to have adequate liquidity may result in having to sell (liquidate) one or more of your assets to pay such taxes. This is probably one of the most important reasons for using insurance to pay estate taxes. Such forced sales could result in a substantially less return than fair market value. Since the insurance trust excludes the insurance from estate taxes, the entire amount of the insurance proceeds can be used towards the tax payment.

Upon your death, the trustee (most likely your child or children) may use the funds from the insurance trust to buy illiquid assets, such as corporate stock or real estate, from the estate. This is called a tax-neutral exchange, meaning that no tax is due because of this asset shift. Another solution is for the trust to loan money to the estate, secured by the estate's assets. Either way, the estate will have the necessary liquidity to pay estate taxes. The trustee can then distribute the trust's assets to the trust's beneficiaries. Thus, your heirs keep full control over the family assets while all the life insurance proceeds are used to pay estate tax and other death costs.

Of course, one of the primary objectives in taking out a life insurance policy is to provide for your surviving spouse and children. The insurance trust is designed to provide income to your spouse for life. Upon the death of a spouse, the insurance company pays the trustee of the insurance trust the value of the policy. The trustee can then make investments with these funds, the income from which is paid to your surviving spouse.

Suppose you owned quite a bit of stock in Kentucky Fried Chicken. Well, out come the reports on cholesterol and suddenly your stock loses most of its value (this is before they come out with KFC Skin Free). So the size of your estate diminishes greatly. In such a situation, your surviving spouse has the option of borrowing against the insurance. The insurance proceeds are not subject to federal estate taxation. After the death of the surviving spouse, the proceeds from the insurance in the insurance trust can be distributed.

The insurance proceeds are not subject to federal estate taxation.

In recent years, "joint survivor" or "second to die" insurance has become very popular and useful. This policy focuses on the death of the surviving spouse. With the estate tax law change in 1981 that increased the marital deduction from 50% to 100% or unlimited, estate tax planning for married couples focused on the second death. That is, with proper planning, estate taxes on the first spouse's death can be eliminated. Joint survivor insurance insures both spouses, is not paid until the surviving spouse dies, and has the advantages of considerably reduced premiums (sometimes less than half of the cost of insuring one spouse) and being obtainable even when one spouse is not insurable.

This policy can fit in very well with an insurance trust or a wealth replacement trust.

There are two appropriate guidelines to remember when considering whether an insurance trust would be beneficial for your estate: 1) If the total value of your estate, including insurance, does not exceed the tax exemption of $600,000 for single individuals and $1.2 million for married couples, your living trust should be named the beneficiary of your insurance policies; and 2) if the assets of your estate, including insurance, do exceed the federal estate tax equivalent exemption, the insurance trust could be a valuable part of your estate plan with regards to avoiding estate taxes on the insurance proceeds.

The trustors, or creators, of the insurance trust should not also be trustees. If they are, then the value of the insurance will be included in their estates and will be taxed. Another family member, a bank trust department, or close friend should be named as trustee, or trustees. In addition, a separate bank account set up to pay the premiums for the insurance in the insurance trust may be helpful.

The trustors of the insurance trust should not also be trustees.

The Wealth Replacement Trust

Another useful tool in reducing estate taxes is the wealth replacement trust. Although it is similar to the living trust, there are three major differences: 1) The wealth replacement trust is non-revocable; 2) you must name an independent trustee to serve as the manager of the wealth replacement trust; and 3) you name somebody else, normally your heirs, to be the immediate beneficiaries of the trust.

After creating the wealth replacement trust, you can transfer up to $10,000 per trust beneficiary per year into the trust without any gift tax ramifications. You transfer the gift to the trust rather than directly to the beneficiary. A notice is given to the beneficiary, giving him or her about 30 days to claim the gift.

You then educate the beneficiary regarding the purpose of the gifting program. As a result, the beneficiary does not claim the gift and the funds are locked into the trust to be managed by the trustee in a prudent manner.

The wealth replacement trust plan may present a problem, however. You may not want to consistently make gifts and, even if you do, $10,000 each year may be too little for your family situation.

To overcome this obstacle, part of the funds can be used to purchase a life insurance policy. Upon your death, or if it is a joint survivor or second to die policy, upon the deaths of both you and your spouse, the life insurance proceeds are paid to the wealth replacement trust, providing more than enough money to pay the tax due.

The wealth preservation trust is non-revocable and generally utilizes an independent trustee.

Many individuals may not have the ability to transfer cash in a gifting program, are uninsurable, or have few or no children to base the gifting program on. There is a program that can overcome these roadblocks.

Wealth Preservation Trusts

The wealth preservation trust is non-revocable and generally utilizes an independent trustee. Unlike the wealth replacement trust

74

and the insurance trust, you are the beneficiary of the income from the trust during your lifetime.

Highly appreciated assets, such as raw land or stock, are transferred into the wealth preservation trust, which provides a tax-free environment. For an asset to qualify for such a transfer, the property cannot already be under a contract for sale and there should not be any substantial debt against it.

Once the transfer is accomplished, the trustee can then sell the asset income tax free, sparing the substantial capital gains if you sold the asset yourself. The proceeds of the sale are reinvested in assets that produce income, which you can receive for life. You also receive an income tax deduction which can be used to reduce the income taxes payable on your income tax return. Thus, the wealth preservation trust places the asset in an estate and income tax free environment, generates income for you and reduces your income taxes. Is there a catch?

After your death, what is remaining in the wealth preservation trust is transferred to the qualified non-profit organization of your choice, rather than going to your children or other heirs, as would be the case in an insurance or wealth replacement trust. However, while you are alive, you retain the right to receive the income, change the manager of the trust, and change the name of the non-profit organization. And if your heirs are concerned about not receiving this asset, perhaps you can set up an insurance trust, funded by life insurance on you. This would replace the asset and not be taxed upon your death.

Children's Trust

The children's trust is an irrevocable trust used to gift assets to your children or grandchildren. It provides for their future education and benefit. In effect, an appreciating asset is removed from your estate and placed into the children's trust. Here the future growth of the asset will remain. For example, suppose you and your spouse were to gift some stock to your children by means of a children's trust. The market value of the stock is expected to increase; hence, that gift is an appreciating asset. By the time of your death, the stock's value could be substantially more. Since the growth of the asset is in the children's estate and not yours, you would reduce the amount of your taxable estate, thus possibly saving a significant amount in estate taxes.

To be sure that the gifted asset is not a part of your estate when you die, you should not name yourself as the trustee of the children's trust. You are effectively gifting to your children or grandchildren your cost basis for that gift. Unfortunately, they do not get the benefit of stepped-up valuation on the gifted assets upon your death.

Spousal Gift

Marvin is a rocket scientist. His wife, Nancy, is a housewife and mother of three. Marvin's estate is worth substantially more than Nancy's because of the way they own assets. If Marvin were to die, after the federal estate tax exemption, Marvin's estate may have to pay estate taxes. If Nancy were to die, and her estate is valued at less than the exemption, the unused part would be lost. Is there a way Marvin and Nancy could better utilize both federal estate tax exemptions? Yes. A spousal gift allows a spouse with a large estate to gift a portion of that estate to the other spouse, who has a very small estate. Though infrequently used, the spousal gift can prove beneficial, depending on the laws of the state. If marital difficulties are a concern, this probably is not a good idea.

To illustrate the possible significance of a spousal gift, take the situation where a husband has an estate valued at $2,000,000, while the wife's estate is valued at zero. With the exemption of $600,000, the husband's taxable estate would be $1.4 million. The estate taxes for his estate are $588,000. However, if the husband were to gift his wife $600,000 (which would be exempted and therefore untaxable), his estate would then be valued at $1.4 million. Less his exemption of $600,000, his taxable estate would then be $800,000. His estate taxes at death are $320,000. Thus, by utilizing the spousal gift, he has saved $268,000 in taxes!

If marital difficulties are a concern, a spousal gift is probably not a good idea.

EXAMPLE	Without Spousal Gift	With Spousal Gift
Husband's Estate	$2,000,000	$2,000,000
Spousal Gift	$0	($600,000)
Exemption	($600,000)	($600,000)
Taxable	$1,400,000	$800,000
Federal Estate Tax	$588,000	**$320,000**

Charitable Remainder Trust

If you have appreciated assets, donating them to a charitable remainder trust can avoid the capital gains tax.

If you have appreciated assets, donating them to a charitable remainder trust can avoid the capital gains tax. You can also receive current tax deductions and a lifetime income. When you give away assets to charity, no gift tax is involved.

Take the example of Mark, who invested $30,000 to help start a video store chain. The video stores multiplied rapidly, and the company is publicly traded. Mark's shares are now worth $1 million. To increase his current income, Mark could sell his shares and buy bonds, but about one-third of the proceeds from the stock sale would be eaten up by capital gains tax. Mark's basis on the stock was $30,000 (the amount he invested). If he had sold those shares for $1 million, he would have a taxable gain of $970,000. With a federal and state tax rate of about 35 percent, he would have owed $340,000 in taxes, leaving him only $660,000 to reinvest.

Instead, Mark has established a charitable remainder trust (CRT), removing $1 million from his estate without incurring a gift tax. A CRT pays income to its beneficiaries as named by the donor. The income can either be for the beneficiary's lifetime or for a fixed term, up to 20 years. A CRT can be an annuity trust, which pays a return that is fixed, but at least 5 percent of the original trust amount. Or, a CRT can be a unitrust, which pays a percentage of the trust assets each year, with 5 percent the minimum.

Since he is giving his stock to charity, Mark will get a charitable deduction. However, since the charity will not receive the money right away, Mark will not get a full $1 million write-off. The IRS uses life expectancy tables to determine when Mark and his wife are likely to die, leaving the trust fund to charity. Making some more complicated calculations, the IRS estimates how much the trust will earn and how much it will pay out. The IRS then projects the amount that will eventually go to charity. The older you are, and the less income you take, the greater the tax deduction to which you are entitled. A tax free insurance trust can purchase life insurance payable to your children. You can make cash gifts to the trust so it can pay the premiums. This will compensate for the assets you have given away.

Charitable remainder trusts can also be used for a donation to a private foundation rather than to a public charity. Or, they can be used as a way to build up a larger retirement fund. Really, CRTs offer so many possibilities for planning that they may seem too good to be true. If you have highly appreciated assets, they are certainly worthy of your consideration.

Charitable remainder trusts can also be used for a donation to a private foundation rather than to a public charity.

CRTs are not for everyone, however. They must be irrevocable. Even the gifts to the trust must be irrevocable. You are giving up full control of the assets placed into the trust, so if things do not go according to plan, you may not obtain the income you desire. You cannot borrow from the fund. In effect, you are limited to the annual income you have agreed upon.

Generation Skipping

For many years, the wealthy have been devising ways to avoid estate and inheritance taxes. One of the most popular strategies was generation skipping. Take the example of Peter, who set up a trust that named his wife and children as beneficiaries during their lifetimes. After they died, his grandchildren were to inherit the trust principal. When Peter died, federal estate taxes were paid from his estate. Not until the death of all his grandchildren, many years in the future, would further tax be owed. Thus, family wealth could be kept intact.

In 1976, however, Congress decided to raise revenues by going after such generation skipping. That law was modified in 1986. Now, generation skipping can be expensive because the estate is taxed twice— the normal estate tax at your death and the generation skipping tax at the death of the skipped individual. The generation skipping tax is at a flat rate of 55% of the amount taxed. Each individual has a $1 million exemption from the generation skipping tax. Thus, a married couple can leave a total of up to $2 million to their grandchildren free of double taxation. Regular federal estate and gift taxes will still be owed.

The generation skipping tax is at a flat rate of 55% of the amount taxed.

SUMMARY

- The $10,000 annual gift exclusion allows you to gift $10,000 per person per year tax-free to as many people as you want.

- The lifetime exemption of $600,000 allows you to gift $600,000 to the individual of your choice, but reduces the death exemption by the same amount.

- Insurance policies are the biggest source of estate tax revenues that the IRS collects.

- For individuals with large estates, the least expensive way to pay taxes may be with insurance.

- Since the insurance trust excludes the insurance from estate taxes, the entire amount of the insurance proceeds can be used towards the tax payment.

- To remove future appreciation from your estate, you may want to give away assets that are likely to appreciate.

- Wealth replacement trusts and wealth preservation trusts can be useful tools in reducing estate and capital gains taxes.

- The spousal gift allows a spouse with a large estate to gift part to the other spouse with a small estate in order to fully utilize both spouse's federal estate tax exemptions.

- Donating appreciated assets to a charitable remainder trust can avoid the capital gains tax.

- A married couple can leave up to $2 million to their grandchildren free from generation skipping tax.

CHAPTER ELEVEN:
ALLOCATION AND DISTRIBUTION OF ASSETS

. . . .

With a will, after probate there is no legal entity left in which to hold your assets. All of the assets in an estate must be distributed outright at the conclusion of the probate process, unless a testamentary trust is established by the will. If you have a living trust, however, your options for allocation and distribution of your assets are unlimited.

Specific Amounts

One such option is leaving specific amounts of distribution or income. Due to inflation, bequests should be specified as a percentage rather than as a fixed amount. For example, you could bequest "5 percent or $10,000, whichever is greater," to your Aunt Millie. Then, if ten years have elapsed and the estate has doubled in value, the 5 percent would be worth $20,000. Or, such $10,000 could shrink in purchasing value to only $5,000 in ten years.

> *If you have a living trust, however, your options for allocation and distribution of your assets are unlimited.*

Unequal Allocation

Unequal allocation, or leaving varying amounts to children, is quite common. There are many situations where unequal allocation may be desirable.

Take, for example, Mark and Marla Higgins' situation. They have two children— their son, who is a very successful business man, and their daughter, who is divorced and has three children. Their allocation heavily favors their daughter, who is most likely to need more funds.

Don and Patsy Hermon have four grown children, one of which is physically disabled. The Hermons chose to have their assets remain in trust to provide for the disabled child as long as she lives. Only after she dies will the Hermons' remaining estate be equally divided and distributed to their three other children.

Micah and Tanera Louis at first chose equal allocation for their two children. However, their eldest son was killed in a work-related accident. His wife and child were well provided for by his company's substantial settlement. Therefore, the Louis' amended their trust to exclude their deceased son and granddaughter.

Dan and Aretha Gibbons have two daughters. Because their eldest married a "warthog-faced buffoon," as Mr. Gibbons put it, he chose to disown her. Aretha, however, still maintained the right to do anything she wanted with her half of the estate. Since she "loves her daughter even if she did marry a bozo," she chose to allocate her half equally to both daughters.

Distribution of Trust Assets

The three most common methods of trust distribution are outright, at a specific age, and deferred distribution.

The three most common methods of trust distribution are outright, at a specific age, and deferred distribution. For minor children, you should consider retaining all assets in trust until the youngest child reaches 21. When all of the assets are in trust, they are available for innumerable unexpected needs, including medical needs. The trust will avoid the need to establish a guardian or conservator through probate court to take care of and administer the funds that might otherwise be necessary to establish until the age of majority, normally eighteen.

Outright distribution does not imply that the assets must be distributed immediately following your death. It simply means that the assets should be distributed within a reasonable period. The successor trustees have the discretion to delay distribution, or sale of the assets, until they deem it appropriate.

Suppose you have named your daughter, Joanne, as a successor trustee (she would also be a beneficiary). At the time of your death, high interest rates may offer a poor market for real estate sales. Thus, Joanne decides it would be more prudent to lease your home and sell it in a more favorable market. Only then would the proceeds of the sale be distributed to the beneficiaries.

Real estate may be distributed simply by rewriting the deed in the name of the beneficiaries.

Rather than liquidating the assets, the trustee may distribute in kind. In other words, real estate may be distributed simply by rewriting the deed in the name of the beneficiaries. Securities, such as stocks, bonds, and mutual funds, can be rewritten in the name of the individual beneficiary. Or assets can be sold and cash distributed. It all depends upon the written direction given in the trust.

For children below the age of eighteen, distribution at a specific age is another form of distribution. If your sixteen-year-old son, Philip, puts every cent he acquires in a bank to save up for college, he is probably mature enough to receive a distribution at the age of eighteen. However, if your eighteen-year-old daughter, Marie, heads to Neiman-Marcus with every paycheck, you may decide to distribute her share at an older age. Some recommend distribution at no earlier than 23. They reason that this gets the children through college and then adds a year or two for the sake of maturity.

With a common type of distribution, deferred distribution, assets are not distributed to your heirs at the time of death. Instead, distribution is delayed for a specific number of years or until the heir reaches a specified age. For example, an heir could receive one-third at 25, one-half at 30, and the rest at 35, effectively distributing one-third at each of these three times. Or, the distribution could be made in increments. One-third could be received outright, one-half in five years, and the remainder in ten years. During the term of the trust, the trustees might also distribute what is necessary for the health, education, support and maintenance of the heir. This is a standard of distribution that is often used and works well in conjunction with lump sum distributions.

With deferred distribution, assets are not distributed to your heirs at the time of death.

The concept behind deferred distribution is that children mature with time. If an heir receives a distribution and frivolously spends the entire amount, he or she later gets a second chance. Most likely, the second time around the heir is much less inclined to unwisely waste the inheritance.

Thus, those who receive their inheritance by means of deferred distribution are less likely to experience what Sharon did. While a sophomore at Princeton, Sharon's parents were tragically killed in a plane crash. Upon receiving a large inheritance in one lump sum, Sharon and two of her friends left school and went on a European shopping spree. Within a matter of months, the money was gone. Perhaps if she had received only one-third of her inheritance outright, another third in five years, and the rest in ten years, the outcome would have been different. Even if she squandered the first third, she may have learned her lesson by the time she received the other distributions.

Income or Distribution?

It may be wise to bequeath to heirs the income derived from your assets, rather than the assets themselves.

In some instances, it may be wise to bequeath to heirs the income derived from your assets, rather than the assets themselves. Suppose your son, Jonathan, is immature and a spendthrift. In such a case, you could retain the assets in the trust and provide "income only" to Jonathon. Your trustee would be authorized to meet emergency needs, such as medical care, educational assistance, etc.

If you have an estate with substantial real estate holdings, you may want to retain these holdings to provide future income for your children. This option is provided with the living trust. The successor trustees maintain the right to buy, sell, borrow against and transfer these assets, for investment purposes.

As you can see, there are many options for distributing your assets. Of course, it is up to you to decide which method is appropriate for each individual child. If you feel your children are fully mature, you may decide to distribute your assets to them outright (all at one time). Perhaps a child is involved with drugs and alcohol. In this instance, it may be appropriate to retain your assets in trust and distribute income only. Another child who is progressing in maturity could receive assets by means of deferred distribution.

Special Situations

In the event one or more of your children fail to survive you, their share of the estate will usually pass to your grandchildren (the children of the deceased child). This is up to you and should be designated in your documents.

For example, consider the Barling family. Bob and Charlotte have two daughters, Dawn and Danielle, each of whom are married and have two children. Upon the death of Bob and Charlotte, half of their assets are to pass to Dawn and half to Danielle. However, suppose Dawn was not living upon her parents' death. Then her share would pass equally to her two children, bypassing her husband. If Dawn and her two children are not alive when Bob and Charlotte die, Dawn's share passes to her sister Danielle, bypassing Dawn's husband.

It is not mandatory to exclude the surviving spouse of a deceased child from distribution.

Note that the spouse is left out. This is the standard method of distribution. That is, distribution is typically along blood lines, including adoption. However, it is not mandatory to exclude the surviving spouse of a deceased child from distribution. You may choose to include the spouse in your living trust.

What will happen to your assets if your children someday get divorced? For one thing, you could leave your assets in trust, with your children receiving income only. Such assets would not be considered the children's property. Thus, the assets in your trust would not be subject to being divided between the divorcing parties. Or, you may choose to leave your assets in trust and have them distributed in five-year increments. In addition, your married children could have their own trusts with separate property agreements. This would ensure that any parental assets passed on to your children will be designated as separate property. In the event there is a divorce, the separate property remains with the individual to whom it belongs. If the children from the marriage remain with the mother, the mother's separate property usually remains hers. However, the court has the right to use the father's separate property for the children.

In the event there is a divorce, the separate property remains with the individual to whom it belongs.

Distributions to Mentally or Physically Handicapped Children

Alex was only sixteen when a motorcycle accident drastically changed his life. Paralyzed from the waist down, he was told he would never walk again. Not only was this news traumatic emotionally, it also proved extremely costly from a financial standpoint. Fortunately, he qualified for governmental assistance. Alex's father, who had passed away years earlier, named him as a beneficiary in his trust. The funds from the trust were to be distributed to Alex when he reached 21. Needless to say, Alex eagerly anticipated his twenty-first birthday. Upon reaching age 21, however, the same government agency that had been assisting Alex financially stepped in and took possession of his entire inheritance!

Do such experiences really happen? In cases such as described above, government agencies may have the right to seize inheritances because government funds have previously been expended on behalf of the handicapped child. What is the solution? The handicapped child could be excluded from directly receiving assets or income. The successor trustee of your trust could be authorized and directed to provide for such a child's welfare, but only in the event government aid does not provide for same. The trustee can directly pay rent, board, education, medical and psychiatric care, transportation, and entertainment without making any direct payment to the child if not paid for by a government agency. Thus, government assistance may not be jeopardized. This is an area of the law that continues to change. You should seek competent advice as to its status when you consider doing this. As time moves along, you should have this provision updated to stay in tune with any changes in the law. As our government needs more funds, it looks with more disfavor on distribution provisions such as this.

Disinheriting

What if you choose to disinherit a child? With a living trust, the solution is very simple. The child who is to be disinherited is excluded as a beneficiary of the trust. Since the trust is a contract, if it does not name a child as a beneficiary, that child is not a part of the trust. No further statement is necessary. To avoid the implication that the child was forgotten, you should name him or her in your pourover will. Suppose you have a will without a living trust. In nearly all states, you can disinherit a child by simply not naming that child as a distributee.

Since the trust is a contract, if it does not name a child as a beneficiary, that child is not a part of the trust.

SUMMARY

- Unequal allocation, or leaving varying amounts to children, is quite common.

- Outright distribution means the assets are available for distribution immediately following your death.

- With deferred distribution, assets are not distributed to your heirs at the time of death; distribution is delayed for a specific number of years or until the heir reaches a specified age.

- If a child fails to survive you, distributions of that child's share of the estate is up to you and should be designated.

CHAPTER TWELVE:
CREATING YOUR ESTATE PLAN

Getting Started

Getting started is quite often the most difficult part of an estate plan. It is best to start now, and then, as time moves along, to modify your plan as necessary to meet your then current goals. If you decide to create a living trust, you need to consider the following decisions:

- Who shall be the trustees?

- Who shall be the executor of your pourover will?

- Who shall be the guardian and conservator, if you have minor or handicapped children?

- To whom shall your assets be left, in what proportion, and when do you want them distributed?

Decisions, Decisions

Rather than making these decisions in a hurried manner, give the alternatives some thought and discussion. It is especially important for a married couple to discuss each potential decision. Then the trust will reflect your mutual desires.

> *Getting started is quite often the most difficult part of an estate plan.*

Presumably, you and your spouse would want to continue to manage your assets; therefore, it is typical to name both spouses as trustees of their living trust. On some rare occasions, such as when one spouse is ill, the other spouse handles everything. In such a situation, it would be appropriate to name only the active spouse as the trustee.

In some instances it may be advisable to name a child (or children) or corporate fiduciary as co-trustee with the surviving spouse. Take, for example, Sam, who is dying of cancer. His wife, Henrietta, getting up in years, has rapidly deteriorating mental faculties. Being concerned about his wife's ability to manage the estate after his death, Sam chooses to name his son, Ralph, as co-trustee. Or, perhaps he needs impartiality, administrative, or investment help. So he decides to name a bank trust department as a co-trustee or the sole trustee.

Successor Trustees

Usually, clients choose one or more of their adult children as successor trustee.

Upon the death, resignation, or incompetence of the surviving spouse, the successor trustee(s) takes over. Usually, clients choose one or more of their adult children (the minimum age is eighteen) as successor trustee. However, anyone you trust may be appropriate, such as a close friend, other close family member, or a corporate fiduciary such as a bank trust department.

Naming an Executor

As you will recall, an executor must also be selected to handle any of your assets that have inadvertently been left outside the trust. This is done with the use of your "pourover" will. For a married couple, the surviving spouse is generally named as the executor. Perhaps the surviving spouse is not physically or mentally able to withstand the eventual appearances in court. Then an adult child, close family member or friend may be more appropriate. For a single person, the successor trustee is typically named as the executor of your will.

Naming a Guardian

With minor or handicapped children, the naming of a guardian is essential. This should be done in your will. If your children are young, it is advisable to also name an alternate guardian. Many years must pass before your children become adults, and in the meantime your guardian could die. For the best protection of your children, it is important to take the time to thoughtfully select a guardian.

If your children are young, it is advisable to also name an alternate guardian.

To Distribute or Allocate?

Unlike a will, the living trust gives each spouse the right to independently determine who is to receive what assets, when and in what proportion. Decisions regarding allocation and distribution of assets need to be made, such as special bequests, equal or unequal allocation, outright, specific ages, income only, or deferred distribution.

Choosing the Appropriate Provisions

Next, you need to select which of the following provisions or additional documents you need:

- Living Will
- Durable Power of Attorney
- Catastrophic Illness Provision
- Transfer of Personal Property
- Appointment of Guardian
- Appointment of Conservator

- Anatomical Gift
- Community or Separate Property Agreements

Each item requires your personal decision and may require reflection and thought before you arrive at the decision that is best for you. Although not every provision may be appropriate for your circumstances, each item does offer desirable legal protection. Your experienced estate planning attorney can provide you with the necessary guidance in creating a plan suitable to your particular needs.

Decisions Pertaining to a Will

If, for whatever reason, you decide that a will is appropriate for your needs, rather than a trust, several factors need to be considered. For example, an executor must be chosen. Because your executor will be handling your personal affairs upon your death, make sure it is someone you trust.

If you have minor children (under 18), a guardian should be determined. For young couples with minor children and a small estate, the use of a "minor children testamentary trust" is beneficial. This trust is established when assets are distributed to it through probate after your death. Thus, this provision assures that management and distribution of your assets are kept away from the court and within your family after initial probate. Thus, the assets you have intended for your minor child or children will be sure to go to them. If you choose to establish a minor children testamentary trust, consideration needs to be given as to who will be the trustees.

CHAPTER THIRTEEN: VISITING THE ATTORNEY

Hopefully this book has helped you review the critical questions and decisions concerning your estate plan. With this in mind, you are prepared to seek out a qualified attorney who is experienced in estate planning. How can you find a competent attorney who specializes in estate planning? The practice of law today, like most things, is very complex. Most state bar exams test on about 20 major areas of the law, estate planning (will, trusts, probate) being one of the areas. As a result, there are few attorneys who specialize or concentrate in the estate planning area. And you should seek a specialist. If you have a heart problem, you visit a heart specialist, not a foot doctor.

Choosing an Attorney

In choosing an attorney, what are some things to avoid? For one thing, make sure you select an attorney, not a financial planner or insurance salesman. You have too much at risk to entrust your estate to someone who is not an attorney.

> *Make sure you select an attorney, not a financial planner or insurance salesman.*

Remember that the price of a trust (or other estate planning documents) is not always indicative of the quality of the trust. You may end up being charged for all of the attorney's time spent to research the provisions that should be included. An experienced attorney is readily familiar with all the viable options. He or she needs only to spend a minimal amount of time (if any at all) in research. Nor is the length of a trust a good indicator. There are many lengthy, disorganized documents out there that do not encompass all the necessary contingencies.

A reliable source for finding a competent attorney in your area is Martindale-Hubbell's Law Directory. Found at your local library, attorneys listed are rated for the quality of their work, their experience, and other factors. I recommend you select a sole practitioner (an attorney who is in practice alone) so you get ongoing personal attention. That way, whenever you call, your attorney will personally address your needs. Whenever you go into the office, you will meet with your attorney, not a junior attorney.

A reliable source for finding a competent attorney in your area is Martindale-Hubbell's Law Directory.

Additionally, select an attorney who practices in your area. If you hire an attorney whose office is an hour's drive away, an unnecessary inconvenience is added. Make sure the attorney you choose is stable and planning to remain in your area for years to come. Then, as time moves along and you have additional needs, questions or problems, you can reach your attorney easily.

Communicate!

Communication between you and your attorney is vital. Some parts of estate planning documents must be written in "legalese" (language that is peculiar to the legal profession). But this does not mean you should not have an accurate understanding of the contents of them. Maybe the document is written so that you cannot understand it. Then a supplemental means of communication, such as a summary written in simple language, should be provided.

Communication is often lacking because the attorney may understand the document, but is unable to simplify or explain it so the client understands it. If the document is organized and a summary is provided, an individual who is not schooled in legal matters can understand it and how it works.

Murphy's Law

It is important to include in your estate plan all the provisions that are needed to encompass every imaginable contingency. In other words, Murphy's Law applies: presume that anything that can happen will happen. Although most of the contingencies (or unexpected occurrences) will never happen to the majority of clients, it is better to be prepared. A good living trust should anticipate every conceivably possible event that may occur for the next ten, twenty, thirty or forty years. Such a comprehensive document only comes from an experienced attorney.

A good living trust should anticipate every conceivably possible event that may occur for the next ten, twenty, thirty or forty years.

What to Ask the Attorney

Well-written, comprehensive documents come only through extensive experience. Therefore, one of the first questions you may ask an attorney is, "How many living trusts do you draw in a year?" This will at least give you a measure of the attorney's experience. The American Bar Association claims that fewer than one percent of the legal fraternity understand the living trust. I urge you to select an attorney who has been planning estates for a number of years. Experience comes naturally through time.

The next logical question may be, "What are your fees?" Make sure they are reasonable in comparison with other competent attorneys in your area.

What is the Structure of a Good Living Trust?

Although the organization and structure of a good living trust will vary, certain provisions are necessary in order to accommodate your changing circumstances. With today's fluctuating economy, you may be in a different financial situation from one day to the next. Some of the trust provisions may not apply at this particular time in your life, but they could apply sometime in the future. That is why they are included.

Living Trust Seminars

What about those free seminars on living trusts that you see advertised? If you decide to attend one, there are a few things you should keep in mind. The living trust fee quoted to you may ultimately be much higher when the cost of additional documents is added. Watch out for firms who tell you it is necessary to have your property inventoried in detail or appraised in order to transfer it into the trust. An appraisal or detailed inventory is normally not necessary and may simply be a way to provide asset information that is used for investment (and commission making) advice.

Watch out for firms who tell you it is necessary to have your property appraised in order to transfer it into the trust.

The Quality of Your Estate Plan is Important

Also, keep in mind that a poorly written trust could put your estate in a worse situation than if you had no trust at all. Even though the main advantage of a living trust is to avoid probate, a trust falls under the legal jurisdiction of the probate code. Thus, any need for clarification of a trust must be handled in the probate courts. So if your trust is poorly written, it may end up in probate court upon your death, with petitions being presented to clarify the trust wording.

A poorly written trust could put your estate in a worse situation than if you had no trust at all.

If you find an attorney who offers a living trust for $495, or some other low figure, you can bet on at least two problems: 1) That he or she will run you and your living trust through the office as fast as possible because of dependence on volume; and 2) you can never be sure what the attorney may be leaving out. A good rule of thumb is: The lower the price of the estate plan, the higher the risk. The many thousands of dollars a mistake in your estate plan could cost far outweigh the added few hundred dollars you invest now with a competent, experienced attorney who will make sure the job is done right.

Remember, your estate is too important to your retirement and to your heirs to put your assets in the hands of someone without much experience. If you don't get the experience you need, someday you or your heirs may be very sorry.

CONCLUSION

Now that you are somewhat familiar with the estate planning alternatives that are available to you, you can make an educated decision. Whether you choose to do nothing, have a will and related documents prepared, or have a living trust drawn up, you should now be more aware of the consequences of your actions. You may, like nearly seventy percent of the adult population in the United States, choose to do nothing. If so, your state government already has a "will" for you— a complicated document that may be to your detriment. Or, you may elect to have your estate go through the frustrating and often expensive probate process. In any event, you should consciously choose an estate plan that is best for you, so that you can keep your assets where you want them.

Don't do like most do— procrastinate. Get started now by scouting out an attorney to help. And set up that first appointment. Make a commitment to yourself that you'll look over your estate within the next two weeks. Otherwise, you might put this information aside and never get back to it. When you make a commitment to yourself and to your family, you take the first step to properly plan your estate. Remember, you spend a lifetime of love and work putting you and your family and material possessions together, maintaining them, nurturing them. Don't let your disability or death destroy this love and hard work!

OTHER BOOKS AVAILABLE FROM
Layman's LawGuides

Divorce and Child Custody: Your Options and Legal Rights, Deanna Peters and Richard L. Strohm, ISBN: 0-9630356-1-4

Understanding Immigration Law: How to Enter, Work and Live in the United States, Nancy-Jo Merritt, ISBN: 0-9630356-2-2

Consumer Rights and Remedies: Legal Tips for Savvy Purchases of Goods, Services and Credit, Marc R. Lieberman, ISBN: 0-9630356-4-9

Protecting Assets With Estate Planning: Wills, Trusts, and Other Legal Options, Donald J. Burris, ISBN: 0-9630356-5-7

Rights in the Workplace: Employee's Guide to Legal Protection, Thomas J. Kennedy and Richard L. Strohm, ISBN: 0-9630356-3-0

Conozca las leyes de inmigración: Sepa como entrar, trabajar y permanecer in Los Estados Unidos, Nancy-Jo Merritt, Abogada (traducción de María Cristina Castro), ISBN: 0-9630356-7-3

Patents, Trademarks and Copyrights: Practical Strategies for Protecting your Ideas and Inventions, David G. Rosenbaum, ISBN: 0-9630356-6-5

Adoption: A Legal Guide for Birth and Adoptive Parents Kelly Allen Sifferman, ISBN: 0-9630356-8-1

Staying Afloat Financially: Legal Tips When Tough Times Hit, Richard L. Strohm, ISBN: 0-9630356-9-X

For copies of the titles listed above, send $12.50 each to:
MAKAI PUBLISHING GROUP
P.O. Box 14213
Scottsdale, AZ 85267-4213

Please send me the titles listed below. I have enclosed $12.50 for each book, which includes shipping and handling. (Or choose any 5 books; pay only $49!)

Qty:	Title:	Qty:	Title:
____	Divorce and Child Custody	____	Conozca las leyes de inmigracion
____	Understanding Immigration Law	____	Patents, Trademarks and Copyrights
____	Consumer Rights and Remedies	____	Adoption
____	Protecting Assets With Estate Planning	____	Staying Afloat Financially
____	Rights in the Workplace		

Name _____

Address _____

City _____ State _____ Zip _____

Telephone ( ) _____

NOTES

NOTES

NOTES